Cambridge E

Elements in Musi
edited k
William A. E
University of Missouri–Kansas City

WEST SIDE STORY
IN SPAIN

*The Transcultural Adaptation of an
Iconic American Show*

Paul R. Laird
University of Kansas

Gonzalo Fernández Monte
Independent Scholar

CAMBRIDGE
UNIVERSITY PRESS

CAMBRIDGE
UNIVERSITY PRESS

University Printing House, Cambridge CB2 8BS, United Kingdom

One Liberty Plaza, 20th Floor, New York, NY 10006, USA

477 Williamstown Road, Port Melbourne, VIC 3207, Australia

314–321, 3rd Floor, Plot 3, Splendor Forum, Jasola District Centre,
New Delhi – 110025, India

103 Penang Road, #05–06/07, Visioncrest Commercial, Singapore 238467

Cambridge University Press is part of the University of Cambridge.

It furthers the University's mission by disseminating knowledge in the pursuit of
education, learning, and research at the highest international levels of excellence.

www.cambridge.org
Information on this title: www.cambridge.org/9781108970457
DOI: 10.1017/9781108980722

© Paul R. Laird and Gonzalo Fernández Monte 2022

First published 2022

A catalogue record for this publication is available from the British Library.

ISBN 978-1-108-97045-7 Paperback
ISSN 2631-6528 (online)
ISSN 2631-651X (print)

West Side Story in Spain

The Transcultural Adaptation of an Iconic American Show

Elements in Musical Theatre

DOI: 10.1017/9781108980722
First published online: June 2022

Paul R. Laird
University of Kansas

Gonzalo Fernández Monte
Independent Scholar

Authors for correspondence: Paul R. Laird, kuvillancico@gmail.com;
Gonzalo Fernández Monte, gonzalo.fm@outlook.es

Abstract: *West Side Story* first became famous in Spain when the Robert Wise film opened there in 1962, and the version remained popular for decades. Brief international tours came to various cities in Spain in the 1980s, but their presence did not diminish memory of the film, which had a major influence on the country's first stage adaptation of the show in 1996. Directed by Ricard Reguant and produced in Barcelona by Focus, the production also toured. After another international tour played in three Spanish cities in summer 2009, the Madrid company SOM Produce mounted a rendition in 2018 directed and choreographed by Federico Barrios, the first Spanish stage version based on the original 1957 staging. This Element compares the adaptations of the 1996 and 2018 versions in detail, illuminating issues encountered when translating a musical for another culture.

Keywords: Leonard Bernstein, Stephen Sondheim, musical theatre, Anglo-American musical, *West Side Story,* Spain, adaptation/translation, Broadway

ISBNs: 9781108970457 (PB), 9781108980722 (OC)
ISSNs: 2631-6528 (online), 2631-651X (print)

Contents

Introduction

American musicals occupy a place of prominence in worldwide culture, being an effective vehicle for the communication of ideas and a powerful part of the entertainment industry. Though many works that premiere on Broadway never leave the United States, some manage to cross national borders and find success in other countries, generating intense reactions, stirring debate on artistic forms or social issues, and even redefining the local leisure economy. *West Side Story* was one of these works. Created by a team of first-rate artists – Jerome Robbins, Leonard Bernstein, Stephen Sondheim, and Arthur Laurents – the show's Broadway premiere in 1957 was a turning point for musical theatre, a notable achievement in the use of the genre's forms of communication to narrate drama and offer social commentary. Another ground-breaking aspect of the show was the innovative and expressive use of dance. *West Side Story* has reached many corners of the world, largely from the popularity of Robert Wise's film adaptation from 1961, but also in countless stage productions and revivals.[1] Our analysis focuses on the reception, cultural adaptation, and general impact of *West Side Story* in Spain, a country that has embraced the Anglo-American musical as a significant part of its entertainment industry.

From the first reports of the Broadway premiere of *West Side Story* in the Spanish press, this musical has stood out for its rich presence in Spain, spanning more than sixty years. Highlights of this include the extraordinary reception of the first cinematic version when it came to Spain in 1962, the visits of touring companies, development of two new productions in 1996 and 2018, and the very recent reception of the new cinematic adaptation. The same property manifested in different versions is consistent with the life of most musical theatre works, subject to transformation over the years to different formats, historical periods, staging possibilities, new audiences, and diverse cultural contexts. Our Spanish case study is a splendid example of this phenomenon, revealing how a show born in the 1950s as a musical theatre piece of Shakespearean origin with a focus on specific American social issues works its way through the decades in different contexts, speaking to several Spanish generations.

The history of *West Side Story* in Spain is part of a long, prolific presence of the Anglo-American musical in this country. Though there were attempts to produce American musical theatre works early in the twentieth century, the

---

[1] According to the Library of Congress, 'There are more than 250 domestic productions every year and the libretto has been translated into over 26 languages, including Chinese, Hebrew, Dutch, and six separate Spanish translations'. '*West Side Story*: Birth of a Classic'. Library of Congress [website]. www.loc.gov/exhibits/westsidestory/westsidestory-legacy.html, accessed 12 July 2021.

genre started to become established in Spain in the 1950s and 1960s, during Franco's dictatorship. The American musical was a progressive form of theatre that the Spanish accepted as desirable entertainment for popular, mass audiences. In this sense, it replaced other genres that had performed the same function in other moments of Spanish history – most notably the zarzuela, that by then many considered a dated, decadent genre.[2] Many works of Anglo-American musical theatre have been produced in Spain, some leaving a deep impression, like the first local production of *Jesus Christ Superstar* in 1975, a revival of *Man of La Mancha* in 1997, or *The Lion King*, which premiered in Madrid in 2011 and remains on the boards – the nation's longest-running production of a musical.[3] The main centres for the genre in Spain have always been the two largest cities, Madrid and Barcelona, and many productions tour the country before or after establishing themselves in one of these two places.

Though local artists have been creating original musicals throughout the last few decades, adapting Anglo-American works remains the most common source for productions in Spain. Almost every version of such a show includes a rendition of the entire text into *castellano* – or *català* when premiered in Barcelona.[4] A common procedure in the production of musicals in different countries, a text's adaptation reveals many interesting details of the consequences of such a transfer to different cultural contexts. Realising song lyrics in another language poses an artistic and aesthetic challenge. Also, shows with a deep social message like *West Side Story* require great care to be understood fully by – and made relevant to – new audiences. We explore these aspects in this Element through a comparative analysis of the two adaptations of the show into *castellano* that have been produced in Spain.

This Element is divided into seven sections in which we examine in chronological order several manifestations of *West Side Story* in Spain. Section 1 deals with

---

[2] Mateo ('Anglo-American musicals', pp. 331–2) explains how Anglo-American musicals began to satisfy some cultural needs no longer fulfilled in Spain by the opera, zarzuela, or *revista*.

[3] The growth of the Anglo-American musical as a genre for entertainment in Spain started slowly in the 1950s and began to grow substantially in the 1970s. Sources that cover the phenomenon include: Santamaría and Martínez, *Desde* Al Sur del Pacífico *hasta* Más allá de la Luna*: casi 6 décadas de teatro musical en España* and Mia Patterson, *75 Años de historia del musical en España (1930–2005)*. The authors of this current Element are also in the process of a larger research project on this topic.

[4] Spanish, like many languages, has numerous dialects. *Castellano* is the version of Spanish that originated in the medieval Kingdom of Castile. The term now refers to the dialect spoken in Spain as opposed to various versions spoken in the Americas, though it can also indicate the use of Spanish in more specific areas of the country, such as in the northern and central regions. In Spain both terms, *español* and *castellano*, are used to refer to the common language of the country, but the former can be controversial when mentioned in relation to other co-official languages of certain regions, like *català* or *galego*. In this sense, *castellano* is popularly considered the preferred choice.

the first reactions to the work in the 1950s and 1960s, especially the film's reception. Sections 2 and 4 focus on touring productions of *West Side Story* that visited Spain in the 1980s and 2000s, respectively. Sections 3 and 5 approach the history of productions that premiered in Barcelona in 1996 and in Madrid in 2018. The sixth section is a thorough analysis of the adapted text for these two productions compared with the original work. Section 7 examines the reception of the 2021 film.

We thank series editor William A. Everett and Cambridge University Press for their interest in this project and for their advice and assistance. Thanks to Federico Barrios, José María Cámara of SOM Produce, Focus S.A., Ricard Reguant, Albert Mas-Griera, and David Serrano for providing valuable information and material. Paul Laird thanks his wife, Joy, for abiding his lifelong obsession with *West Side Story* and for her constant love and support. Gonzalo Fernández thanks his family, especially his husband, José, for always supporting and sharing his passion for musicals.

Permissions

The authors received permission from both Albert Mas-Griera and David Serrano to quote their adaptations of *West Side Story* for the purpose of analysing and comparing their work.

Figures 1–4 were reproduced from the covers of publications in the collection of Gonzalo Fernández Montes.

Figures 5–7 and 9–11 are photos taken by Javier Naval for SOM Produce, offered for free use and reproduction on their website.

Figure 8 is a photo taken by Paul R. Laird

1 First Encounters of *West Side Story* with Spanish Culture in the 1950s and 1960s

'A New Form of Dramatic Art'

Although *West Side Story* would not be performed in Spanish theatres until a quarter of a century after its Broadway premiere, the Spanish media covered this musical's huge impact in theatrical culture from its first productions, and Spain embraced it as an exceptional work.

In order to appreciate this phenomenon of reception one must understand that around 1960 Spain had limited access to American musicals. The country was submerged in the Francoist dictatorship, a period of cultural isolation. Nevertheless, in the 1950s and 1960s the regime went through a stage of international openness (*aperturismo*) that facilitated the entry of American theatrical works. In 1955 *Al Sur del Pacífico* (an adaptation of Rodgers and Hammerstein's *South Pacific*) premiered in Madrid, the first production of an

Anglo-American musical in Spain in twenty years. During the 1960s, there were more productions of Broadway musicals in Madrid and Barcelona. Celebrated works like *Oklahoma!* and *My Fair Lady* had not yet arrived in Spain, but their international success was known by some experts in the field. Numerous shows arrived in the country as films.

In the years before the *West Side Story* film premiered in Spain, some journalists came to know the show by attending productions in New York (1957, revived 1960), London (1958), and Paris (1961). Among the first reviews of the original production in the Spanish press was one by Gustavo Puiche for the newspaper *La Hora*. This correspondent described a show that 'arrives at the stage with the aspiration of passing as the first work of a new theatrical genre. ... a new "thing", perfectly developed and bearing every luxury', whose great achievement was a convincing mixture of distinct elements from several theatrical genres: drama, tragedy, opera, and ballet. Puiche also declared that, should *West Side Story* play in Spain, the response might be as fervent as on Broadway.[5] Reviewing the West End production for the Francoist newspaper *Falange*, Guy Bueno also praised the innovations that *West Side Story* brought to the musical theatre:

> We stand before something completely new, as if witnessing the birth of a new form of dramatic art.
>
> For the first time, Americans have transferred tragedy to the music hall stage. The result is surprising, moving, and convincing at the same time.
>
> What's the reason for this extraordinary success? It is no doubt the poetry contained in the work, which is found – perhaps not surprisingly – more in the dances than in the song lyrics.[6]

In 1961, producer Felix Marouani took *West Side Story* to continental Europe with a successful touring production that premiered in Paris's Alhambra Theatre in March and toured in numerous other cities. The production used the original English text and pursued the initiative, uncommon at the time, of projecting titles on a screen in the local language.[7] Federico García-Requena, correspondent for *Blanco y Negro*, reviewed the production after attending one of the Parisian performances. He highlighted Jerome Robbins's work as creator of a choreographic style then unknown in the French capital, characterised by a perfect coordination between dance and theatrical action. García-Requena also found innovative qualities in *West Side Story*:

---

[5] Puiche, 'El último estreno', p. 15.

[6] Bueno, '*West Side Story*', p. 5. There is unfortunately not enough space in this Element to provide the original Spanish text from each of these reviews.

[7] 'France', p. 41.

Paris has just discovered a new form of spectacle, . . . a revolutionary mixture of opera, operetta, musical comedy, ballet, review, concerto . . . a little bit of everything, but so wisely seasoned, that it is a pure delight for the spectator. . . . We stand before a completely original show that sums up, we may say, what we could call the total theatre.[8]

Love Without Barriers

If the first theatrical productions of *West Side Story* had dazzled Spanish reviewers who saw them, the impact caused by the cinematic version co-directed by Robert Wise and Jerome Robbins was similar. The film premiered in the United States in October 1961 and took more than a year to arrive in Spanish cinemas, but its fame had already spread worldwide thanks to its resounding success at the Academy Awards in April 1962, where the film won in ten categories, including Best Picture.[9]

After viewing the film in Paris, García-Requena praised it effusively in an extensive five-page report for *Blanco y Negro* magazine:

It has been said again and again that *West Side Story* is a happy discovery of 'total spectacle'. A serious play mixed with songs and dances that are uniquely performed by some thirty young people selected and trained to the maximum, with no small mistakes that break the magic of the film's charm from the start to the end. A rare example of perfection, that far surpasses the genre of *Singin' in the Rain*, providing the impression that we stand before a new cinematic era that will have continuity and serve as an indisputable beacon for the current generation of *metteurs en scène*.

From *West Side Story* a new cinematic style of true impact has been born: alive, dynamic, overwhelming and modern to the bone.[10]

Spanish writer and philosopher Julián Marías, who had previously attended a theatrical performance of *West Side Story* in New York, also praised the cinematic version, which he saw in Buenos Aires. In an inspired article for the *Gaceta Ilustrada*, Marías commented on the effectiveness of the film's artistic resources as a vehicle for confronting the social issue that it portrays. He observed that, thanks to the cinematic version, a property that in theatre was no more than 'a show for minorities' (meaning 'for the few') could now be experienced on screens around the world and exert a strong influence on the thinking of young people. Marías praised *West Side Story* as a decisive step forward:

---

[8] García-Requena, 'Romeo y Julieta', pp. 40, 42.
[9] *West Side Story* still holds the record for most Oscars obtained by a musical film.
[10] García-Requena, '*West Side Story*', pp. 46, 48.

Figure 1 Program of *West Side Story*, designed in 1962 for its projection in Spanish cinemas.

It is a major showcase of what an art form can be in which the various skills are not joined or juxtaposed, but merged into a *superior* unity, into a more complex and richer art. *West Side Story*, which I thought was a revelation of what the theatre can become … has now, as a film, moved forward no less than the limits of cinema.[11]

---

[11] Marías, '*West Side Story*', p. 23.

The first screening of the film in Spain took place on 7 December 1962 at the Aribau Cinema in Barcelona, serving as the opening engagement for the venue. Businessman Pedro Balañá ambitiously announced that it was 'the most modern cinema in the world'.[12] The screening of *West Side Story* in the Cine Paz of Madrid began on 1 March 1963, running simultaneously with the one in Barcelona; and until the end of that year the film only appeared in those two Spanish cities, 'given the extraordinary features' of the film.[13] This advertising claim referred to the technical prerequisites for projecting the film, only possible in those venues blessed with the latest equipment.[14] Thanks to the critical raves and huge success with the audience, the film had an uninterrupted record run in both cinemas. Almost five months after the Barcelona premiere, a reporter from *El Mundo Deportivo* described the film's place of privilege in Spanish culture:

> In a short time the film will have run for twenty weeks, an unprecedented length in our city [Barcelona] over many years. This exceptional event matches the immense popularity that we have found in the melodies, characters, and situations from *West Side Story*. Natalie Wood, Richard Beymer, Rita Moreno, George Chakiris, and Russ Tamblin have become favourites of our audience, and every mouth and heart sing the marvelous songs 'Maria' and 'Tonight', for example, that are already representative of our time.
>
> From everywhere in Cataluña, as well as from other regions, many people come to see *West Side Story*. Because it is, undoubtedly, and with an absolute unanimity, the most sensational, wonderful, and moving spectacle developed in our time.[15]

West Side Story remained a favourite subject in Spanish news for months. In the seventh presentation of the Premios San Jorge de Cinematografía (prizes awarded by the Barcelona delegation of Radio Nacional de España), held in October 1963, this film received the San Jorge Great Prize and prize for Best Foreign Film.[16] In celebration of the film running for one year at the Aribau Cinema, on 9 December 1963, they gave free tickets for that night's screening to every audience member named Antonio or Maria.[17] The Paz Cinema, for its part, celebrated its first anniversary of presenting *West Side Story* by inviting George Chakiris to Madrid, who also visited Barcelona.[18]

---

[12] Martínez Tomas, 'Inauguración de *Aribau-Cinema*', p. 45.

[13] 'Aribau Cinema. 8 semanas clamorosas', p. 11.

[14] The film was in the new Panavision 70 mm format, with the Todd-AO 6-track sound system.

[15] 'Desde hace casi cinco meses, un éxito sensacional', p. 10.

[16] 'Los Premios San Jorge de Cinematografía 1962', p. 36.   [17] 'Primer aniversario', p. 11.

[18] Peñafiel, 'George Chakiris', p. 19; 'El domingo llegará', p. 8.

Screenings at the Paz ceased on 1 April 1964. The film had started to be shown in other cities, touring the country over the next several months.[19] In the Aribau Cinema, *West Side Story* ran without interruption for a total of 96 weeks; in this venue alone, almost 800,000 spectators saw it.[20] A year after the Barcelona premiere, José Sagré of *El Mundo Deportivo* explained that the key to this success lay in the film's ability to satisfy all audiences:

> [W]e stand before a really exceptional film that pleases Tyrians and Trojans, that is, those that show a rigid intransigence on matters of quality, and those who simply desire entertainment and fun, with no further worries, that is to say, the majority audience that, at the end of the day, we have to admit, is unique in making possible such really fabulous successes.[21]

From the beginning of its viewing in Spain, the title assigned to the film in Peru and Argentina (where it had premiered in April and May 1962, respectively), *Amor sin barreras* (*Love Without Barriers*), was added in parentheses after the original title, but it was the English one – *West Side Story* – that stayed as the main title and became famous in Spanish culture.[22] For a year and a half the film showed only in its original version with Spanish subtitles, an unusual decision in a country where it has long been the practice to dub foreign language films, and a wise one according to a critic of the daily *Marca*: 'dubbing is really not necessary, because the few dialogues are perfectly understandable with the titles';[23] in the review cited above, Sagré also emphasised that 'dialogues were not needed because everything is stated without confusion by means of the dance, gestures, expressions, rhythm and realistic sets themselves that express the atmosphere of lyric tragedy'.[24] Nevertheless, on 2 June 1964, the Aribau Cinema started screening a dubbed version with spoken dialogues in Spanish, leaving the songs in English with subtitles, as is customary with musical films in Spain. According to a reviewer for *El Mundo Deportivo*, 'the average spectator feels more on his turf when hearing the characters speaking our language, and it even seems to present the Puerto Ricans more effectively'.[25]

---

[19] Consulted reviews demonstrate that the film arrived in Asturias in December 1963, to Almería and Granada in March 1964, to the Canary Islands in July 1964, and to Mataró and Sabadell (province of Barcelona) in February 1965.

[20] Proud of this historical achievement, the Aribau Cinema celebrated its 50th anniversary in 2012 with a screening of *West Side Story*. The Paz Cinema also chose this iconic title, among others, to celebrate its 75th anniversary in 2018. See '*West Side Story* vuelve al cine' and 'Cine Paz celebra'.

[21] Sagré, '*West Side Story*: La película', p. 8.

[22] The title *Amor sin barreras* was adopted in Mexico and Portugal (translated to *Amor sem barreiras*, in the latter case) when the film premiered in these countries in April 1963. See '*West Side Story* (1961): Release Info'.

[23] Paul, '*West Side Story*', p. 10.   [24] Sagré, '*West Side Story*: La película', p. 8.

[25] C. 'Versión española', p. 5.

Even in the first months, Spanish cinemas advertised *West Side Story* as 'The film with ten Oscars', 'The triumph of the 20th Century cinema',[26] and 'A total and ultimate spectacle'.[27] Many press reviews – which kept appearing until the beginning of 1965, as the film reached new venues throughout the country – unanimously and unreservedly praised it.[28] In an extensive collection of articles about the film by several authors published in the magazine *Film Ideal* (see Figure 2), Munsó Cabús declared that:

> [*West Side Story*] is a report, a social testimony, a realistic painting, an opera and a *ballet*, everything in a single piece. However, what's truly extraordinary, what leads us undoubtedly to admiring delirium, is that every one of those facets of man's creative expression finds an incredible, almost inexplicable balance and homogeneity.[29]

Much of the critical praise focused on Jerome Robbins's work, as well as the lead actors, especially Natalie Wood. Only a few reviewers commented on the music.[30] Some authors commented on the plot's social significance. María Nieves González from the magazine *Primer Plano* identified a 'double edge' in *West Side Story*'s success, noting that the creators had enriched themselves with an aesthetically appealing image of juvenile delinquency.[31] In the daily *Proa*, Enrique Fernández reflected upon the social predicament portrayed in the work, declaring that the cultural values of 'antiquated Europe' did not allow for juvenile delinquency to reach the grave depths observed in America.[32] It is worth mentioning that both publications were Falangist, aligned to the political doctrines of Franco's dictatorship. In any case, there was a unanimous opinion that the show's authors had succeeded in integrating the tragedy *Romeo and Juliet* into a truthful, modern picture, approaching the genres of documentary and realistic cinema.

Some critics noted that the film *West Side Story* represented not only a step forward in the broad history of cinematography, but also specifically for film musicals.[33] They believed that the genre stagnated after the creations of the great directors Stanley Donen, Gene Kelly, and Vincent Minnelli: 'Apart from

---

[26] 'Aribau Cinema. 8 semanas clamorosas', p. 11.   [27] 'Cinema Paz: *West Side Story*', p. 28.

[28] Among many such reviews, one might consult: Sagré, '*West Side Story*, gigantesco espectáculo'; Avello, 'Real Cinema'; García Jiménez, '*West Side Story*, un film'; and Marin-Hidalgo, 'La opinión del crítico'.

[29] Moya *et al.* 'Nada más que la verdad', p. 190.

[30] R. T. '*West Side Story*', p. 4; Fernández-Cid, 'Discos: Dos publicaciones', p. 116; Moya *et al.* 'Nada más que la verdad'.

[31] González Echevarría, '*West Side Story*', p. 3.   [32] Fernández, 'Tema y pensamiento', p. 7.

[33] Villegas, 'Ante *West Side Story*', pp. 178–9; Guarner, Parejo-Díaz, Cobos, and Munsó Cabús in Moya *et al.* 'Nada más que la verdad', pp. 186–90; A. Q. '*West Side Story* (Capitol)', p. 4.

Figure 2 Cover of the magazine *Film Ideal* 116 (15 March 1963), with a *West Side Story* illustration by famous Spanish painter José Ramón Sánchez.

the classical titles, musical [cinema] doesn't exist.'[34] *West Side Story* could be seen as a possible revitalisation of the classic film musical:

> [T]he ten Oscars of *West Side Story* ... officially acknowledge, for the first time, that a story can be told through drama, music, and dance, with perfectly

---

[34] Villegas, 'Ante *West Side Story*', p. 178.

vulgar and everyday characters and sets. We had known this for a long time, since *On the Town* . . .; but the important thing is now for the mass audience to discover this, the same audience that can resurrect the genre with their support.[35]

Praise for *West Side Story* as a fresh influence was not limited to the field of cinema: Díez-Crespo, who years before had referred to the Madrid production of *Al Sur del Pacífico* as a worthy model for the decadent Spanish lyric theatre, also identified *West Side Story* as evidence that contemporary musical theatre was in good health:[36]

There's a clear example that demonstrates that the musical, lyric genre, zarzuela, whatever you wish to call it, is not in decadence and progresses with the times. These days the film – previously a musical tragedy – *West Side Story* is being screened in Madrid. Is this not a lyrical genre? Then let it serve as a model. At least, when someone thinks or talks about the lyrical genre and its validity or decadence, make sure to consider this musical work.[37]

As a final example of the film's influence on Spanish culture, *West Side Story* might have exerted a strong influence on the film *Los Tarantos* directed by Francisco Rovira-Beleta, which premiered in 1963 and achieved notoriety for its Academy Award nomination in the Best Foreign Language Film category. *Los Tarantos* offered another contemporary rethinking of *Romeo and Juliet*, taking place among two gypsy families from a neighbourhood in Barcelona, and with musical scenes of *flamenco*. *Los Tarantos* has been repeatedly described as 'a Spanish *West Side Story*'.[38]

Beyond the Movie Theatres

A study on the reception of *West Side Story* in 1960s Spain would not be complete without mentioning dissemination of its songs through live concerts and recordings. Spaniards were familiar with the songs, even before it was possible to watch the film without travelling to Barcelona or Madrid, because of concerts, recordings, and the important effects of radio and television.

The versatility of Bernstein's music allowed a great number of artists who performed in various styles to include songs or instrumental selections from the show in their repertories. Many of these versions arrived in Spain through the recording market. Instrumental and symphonic music lovers could purchase excerpts from *West Side Story* recorded by US pianists Ferrante and Teicher

---

[35] Guarner in Moya *et al.* 'Nada más que la verdad', p. 188.

[36] As stated above, the zarzuela had fallen into decadence, and there was an intense debate taking place in Spain on the present and future of musical theatre, a topic that exceeds the scope of this work.

[37] Díez-Crespo, 'Crítica de teatro', p. 42.   [38] Crowther, 'Gypsies and Flamenco'.

(published in Spain by United Artists in 1961), Franck Pourcel and his Grand Orchestra (La Voz de Su Amo, 1964), the Command All Stars Orchestra (Hispavox, 1966), the Boston Pops (RCA Victor, 1967), and the New Westminster Orchestra (Mercury, 1968). Jazz aficionados could enjoy Buddy Rich's disc (Liberty, 1966). Sammy Davis, Jr recorded a medley of songs from the show (Reprise Records, 1967). In various pop genres, many artists included versions of 'Maria', 'Tonight', 'Somewhere', and 'America' in their discographies, including: Andy Williams (CBS, 1962), Trini López (Hispavox, 1964), The Shadows (La Voz de Su Amo, 1964), Cliff Richard (La Voz de Su Amo, 1965), The Brothers Four (CBS, 1965), and Shirley Bassey (La Voz de Su Amo, 1967). The film's soundtrack was issued in Spain by CBS in 1962.

Some Spanish artists also recorded versions of songs from *West Side Story* throughout the 1960s, including early adaptations of the texts into *castellano* and *català*. Composer, arranger, and conductor Augusto Algueró, from Barcelona, wrote adaptations in *castellano* of 'Maria' and 'Tonight' that were published in 1962 – before the film's premiere in Barcelona – released in versions by Mexican singer Alejandro Algara (Zafiro, 1962),[39] the singer Michel from Alicante (Columbia, 1962), and the Latin Combo from Catalonia (Vergara, 1962; only 'Maria').

Canciones del Mundo published Algueró's adaptations in 1962 in piano/ vocal and band arrangements.[40] The first pages of the scores include mention of the film and some of the recordings released in Spain. Algueró's adaptations of the texts are faithful to the original meaning. In 'Maria', he respected the poetic tone of the English lyrics and realised some beautiful phrases, such as 'Maria, my life is named Maria' and 'Maria: sweet music of bells / that is a prayer when you say it softly. / Maria, a verse that is life: Maria'.[41] 'Tonight' appeared under the title '¡Qué noche!' ('What a night!'); the English lyric written in the score emanates from Sondheim's lyrics for Tony and Maria in the 'Tonight Quintet'. Algueró first translated the word 'Tonight' as '¡Mirad!' ('Look!') and, at the end of the strophe, as '¡Amor!' ('Love!');[42] we will see in later sections that future adaptations by Mas-Griera and Serrano also use 'amor' as a substitute for 'tonight'.

---

[39] This renowned tenor traveled to Spain that year to take part in the Festival de la Costa Verde de Gijón, taking advantage of his stay to record two discs for the label Zafiro (Matas, 'Madison Spain's' and 'Duo Dinamico').

[40] In Michel's recording and in the scores for voice and piano, Algueró used his pseudonym 'C. Mapel'.

[41] 'Maria, mi vida se llama Maria'; 'Maria: dulce música de campanas / que es un rezo al decirlo en voz baja. / Maria, un verso que es vida: Maria'. Bernstein; Sondheim, 'María'.

[42] Bernstein; Sondheim, '¡Qué noche!'.

Salvador Escamilla, a singer from Barcelona, released the EP *Canta les cançons de West Side Story* (Ediphone, 1963) with versions in *català* of 'Maria', 'Cool', 'Tonight', and 'Somewhere', proving that some words of the original text are more easily adapted into this language than into *castellano*. For example, in 'Cool' the word 'noi' is used for 'boy', which not only preserves the original meaning but also its sonority; on the first notes of 'Tonight' was inserted the expression 'Aquesta nit' (literally 'Tonight'), and in 'Somewhere' the expressions 'un lloc' and 'un temps' easily replace 'a place' and 'a time', providing the same exact meanings and the same number of syllables.

In 1964 it was the turn of the song 'America', published by Canciones del Mundo in arrangements for voice and piano, rock band, and brass band, the text again adapted by Algueró under the pseudonym C. Mapel. Although the adaptation omitted the entire introductory section, it faithfully followed the original text, and preserved its construction as a dialogue, which in the arrangements for band was noted as alternation between a 'girl' and a 'boy'.[43] The musical arrangements, however, were written in 4/4 (instead of the original 6/8 with hemiola) and with the tempo indications 'Tpo. de Twist' (arrangement for voice and piano) and 'Tpo. de Surf' (for rock band and brass band). The bands Conjunto Lone Star (Barcelona; La Voz de Su Amo, 1964) and Los Pekenikes (Madrid; Hispavox, 1964) recorded versions of the song partially observing Algueró's adaptation.[44] The cover by Lone Star features an accompaniment in 4/4, similar to that found in the scores and also used by US singer Trini López in his recording (Hispavox, 1964), released that same year. For their part, Los Pekenikes opted to maintain the original 6/8 metre. Still in 1964, iconic singer and *bailaora* Lola Flores recorded a version of 'America' in flamenco style (Belter, 1964), with a new lyric referring to the Roma community.

Although the show did not appear in theatrical form in Spain until the 1980s, one can say that this work had a profound impact in Spanish pop culture, creating a precedent that would resonate two decades later with its first theatrical performance in a Spanish theatre as a part of an international touring production.

2 *West Side Story* in Spain in the 1980s

As famous as the film of *West Side Story* became in Spain, its stage version did not play there until 1983. This was not surprising because an American show that required a large cast that could master the combination of acting, singing,

---

[43] Bernstein; Sondheim, 'América'.

[44] In the recording by Lone Star the adaptation is attributed to C. Mapel, but the text differs from the one published in the musical scores.

and dancing necessary for *West Side Story* likely could not have been assembled in Spain until years later (see comments by Ricard Reguant concerning his auditions in Section 3). Any production of the show in Spain probably would have been an international tour, and the first to visit was led by Austrian producer Till Polla, who months before had produced a revival of *Hair* in Spain. He collaborated with Francisco Bermúdez in offering *West Side Story* for ten days at Madrid's Teatro Monumental, opening on 6 October 1983.[45] The tour already had played in numerous countries.[46] The company assembled in the United States, with Diana M. Corto as Maria, Norman Large as Tony, and Patricia Khoury as Anita.[47] Corto and Large performed in shows on Broadway, including the former's appearance as Francisca and understudy to Maria in a limited run at the New York City Center in spring 1964.[48] Jay Norman, who played Bernardo in that production and danced in the original version of *West Side Story*, was choreographer for the 1983 tour. He based his dances on the original choreography by Jerome Robbins. Other members of the tour's team included music director Brad Carroll, sets by Paul Kelly, costumes by Denise Romano, and lighting by Ruth Roberts. Of those figures, Kelly and Roberts have had Broadway credits. A controversial aspect of the production commented on by several critics was the 'orchestra' of six live musicians with the remainder realised from recordings,[49] an economic choice that would have detracted from the spontaneity of a fully live performance. The cast presented dialogue and songs in English.

Writing in *El País*, Pilar Sierra states that *West Side Story* ' ... is an essentially American show and all of the choreography is based on natural expression and the rhythms of the people'.[50] She incorrectly suggests that Jerome Robbins was the only person in American dance capable of both directing and choreographing a show, a doubling of responsibilities that became increasingly common in the 1960s. Sierra thinks that Diana M. Corto as Maria 'converts Bernstein's songs into Italian opera arias' and although the singer 'possesses a splendid voice ... at times she loses the natural and modern rhythm that drives this entire work'. She approves of Patricia Khoury's work as Anita, such as in 'America', and believes that Norman Large effectively performed the 'difficult role of Tony'. Sierra's conclusion raises a question: 'The lovers of musical comedy should not fail to go to this show, that, with a cheesiness that is

[45] Torres, '"*West Side Story*" se presenta en Madrid'.

[46] Torres, '"*West Side Story*" se presenta en Madrid'.

[47] Santamaría and Martínez, *Desde Al Sur del Pacífico hasta Más allá de la Luna*, 3 vols., vol. 3, p. 1295.

[48] The Broadway credits for various figures offered in the paragraph are derived from www.ibdb .com, accessed 11–13 October 2020.

[49] Torres, '*West Side Story*'.   [50] Sierra, 'Un clásico musical', p. 53.

all its own, retains the original freshness.' Elsewhere, Sierra appreciates the show's essential seriousness, but perhaps she found it a stretch for the genre to include such tragic elements.

Other reviewers were less impressed. Writing for *ABC*, Juan I. Garcia Garzon, describes the performance from two sides: 'Twenty-six years after its premiere, the power of "West side story" continues to live, augmented and tarnished by the singular filters of memory.'[51] He mentions the production's insubstantial sets, which shook noticeably when the actors used them, and criticises the mixture of live music and recordings. He states: 'Aside from these things, the remainder is splendid, with truly outstanding moments ... ', but the music of *West Side Story* is not his favourite. He characterises the songs as 'part of the sentimental patrimony of the 1960s'. 'I Feel Pretty' is clearly too cute for his taste and he describes 'Somewhere' as 'curdled with bitter hope'. Víctor Manuel Burell wrote a pan for *Cinco Días*, finding the dancing 'acceptable' and the only 'passable' voice was that of Maria.[52] He thinks that Patricia Khoury as Anita offered the 'best performance of the night', but he terms the remainder of the show 'deplorable' with lighting being 'the major disaster'. Burell also pans the accompaniment: 'The orchestra, from the pit, imitated the magnificent staves of Bernstein.' Despite the mixed critical reception, however, at least one audience apparently enjoyed it. Fernando Bejarano of *Diario 16* reports a full house that 'applauded with enthusiasm and shouted "*bravos*"'.[53]

Another international touring company of *West Side Story* came to Spain in 1988, playing at Valencia's Teatro Principal from 18 to 21 February and in August in Almería, San Javier (Murcia), and Santander. The producer was the Broadway Musical Company of New York with Kathryn G. McCarthy, director; Jane Setteducato, choreographer; and Peter Crockford, music director. McCarthy and Setteducato based their work on that of Robbins in what they billed as the 'Original Broadway Version'.[54] Principals included Greg Witzany as Tony, Gay Willis as Maria, Michael Gruber as Riff, Alberto Guzmán as Bernardo, and Abby Walker as Anita. Instrumental accompaniment seems to have varied and included use of local talent. The run in Valencia, for example, included the Orquesta Municipal de Valencia.[55] The company later played in Almería at the Festivales Agosto 88 on 12 August, outdoors in the Plaza Vieja. Writing in *La Voz de Almería* before the performance, Virginia Calvache

---

[51] Garcia Garzon, 'Crítica de teatro', p. 77.   [52] Manuel Burell, 'MUSICA MODERNA', p. 23.

[53] Bejarano, '*West Side Story*', p. 40.

[54] In a newspaper advertisement for the Festival Internacional de Santander, during which the show played, Jeffrey Dunn is identified as the director, but this perhaps refers to the Broadway Musical Company rather than the directorship of the production.

[55] Beltran, 'Una compañia de Broadway', *El País*, p. 31.

provided background about the original staging in 1957 while implicitly noting that the audience would know the property better in its cinematic version. She stated: 'For less than 1,000 pesetas [about 6 euros], we will be able to admire live the original soundtrack of the film to which we laugh, some of us are indignant and more than one of us let slip a telltale, furtive tear.'[56] The performance in San Javier, outside of Murcia in southeastern Spain, took place sometime around 12 August. The company appeared in Santander on 18 August, outdoors at the Plaza de Toros, as part of the Festival Internacional de Santander, a series of events throughout the month that included major symphony orchestras from Europe and the United States and other important artists. A critic for *Diario 16* noted that the bullring was about half full and that the show played 'with success', describing the production as 'A simple mounting on a limited stage sufficient to indicate the different situations in this opera', but with only eight musicians in the orchestra.[57] Ricardo Hontañón, writing for the *Diario Montañés*, sensed the audience's mixed feeling, some obviously expecting a more symphonic version or something closer to the film, and the stage was too far from the audience. Hontañón described 'acceptable results' in the acting and dancing, praising romantic leads Mitzany and Willis and the 'effectiveness in the musical ensemble'.[58]

One finds in the Spanish press in the 1980s evidence of interest in Bernstein and his work. Tomás Marco honoured the American composer on his 65th birthday in *Diario 16*.[59] Marco foregrounds *West Side Story* in Bernstein's output, explores other works by him that were not nearly as well known in Spain, and briefly describes Bernstein's television work. Two years later, the composer/conductor's operatic recording of *West Side Story* drew attention in Spain, partly because Spanish tenor José Carreras sang the role of Tony. Gonzalo Alonso reviewed the release for *El País*, stating that 'the composer picked up the baton to record his work just like he saw it, and surely there are notable changes with respect to the traditional version'.[60] When Bernstein turned 70 in 1988, Federico Sopeña profiled him in the *Diario de Mallorca* in January and an unsigned retrospective on his life appeared on Bernstein's birthday in *La Provincia*.[61] The Boston Symphony's concert at Tanglewood celebrating the event ran on Spanish television on 28 August.[62] Evidence of *West Side Story*'s continuing resonance in Spain may be seen in an article on its 1957 premiere in the *Diario de Las Palmas* in April 1988 and an item in August

[56] Calvache, '*West Side Story*', p. 15.   [57] 'La ópera "*West Side Story*"', p. 4.

[58] Quoted in: Santamaría and Martínez, *Desde Al Sur del Pacífico*, vol. 3, p. 1333.

[59] Marco, 'LEONARD BERNSTEIN', p. 15.   [60] Alonso, 'Discos/Comedia musical', p. 7.

[61] Sopeña, 'Bernstein', p. 40; 'Leonard Bernstein mantiene', p. 40.

[62] 'TVE: Homenaje a Bernstein', p. 47.

on the growing importance of Spanish-speaking customers in the United States in *Expansión*, for which the title came from the song 'America': 'Todo es mejor en América'.[63] The continuing presence of Bernstein and *West Side Story* in Spanish culture in the 1980s, driven by international tours and the film's lingering fame, sets the stage for the show's first Spanish production in 1996.

3 Ricard Reguant and Focus's Production (1996)

Production Development

The first Spanish production of *West Side Story* adapted into *castellano* was initiated by Ricard Reguant and the production company Focus. Reguant, a director from Barcelona and important figure in the development of Spanish musical theatre, had already worked in adaptations of Anglo-American musicals like *Godspell* (*Colors bells*, 1979), *They're Playing Our Song* (*Estan tocant la nostra cançó*, 1990), *Snoopy* (1991), and *Blood Brothers* (*Germans de sang*, 1994), each in *català*. The last three had been produced by Focus, one of the earliest Spanish production companies to specialise in Anglo-American musicals – it would also be the first to bring to the country *Rent* (1999). The production of *West Side Story* in 1996 marked Focus's tenth anniversary.

Reguant recounted in his blog the adaptation's development, which started in 1995 with the acquisition of rights under the condition of hiring one of five choreographers authorised by Jerome Robbins.[64] Given the difficulty in fulfilling this requirement, Reguant requested permission to hire a renowned Spanish choreographer, but was turned down. He hired American choreographer Barry McNabb, who later participated in other Spanish musical theatre productions. The creative team was completed with Albert Mas-Griera in charge of the textual adaptation, Miquel Ortega as musical director leading the orchestra Taller de Músics, Joaquim Roy as scenic designer, María Araujo as costume designer, Quico Gutiérrez as lighting designer, and Toni Vila as sound designer.

Auditions started in May 1996, with about 1,200 contestants.[65] Reguant found the general level of candidates disappointing because most lacked the necessary triple training in dance, singing, and acting: 'Many of them master one of these facets but fail in the rest.'[66] At that time, specialised teaching in musical theatre was almost non-existent in Spain. The only documented exceptions are The English Theatre Workshop – a company founded in Madrid in 1993 by English actor and director Gary Willis – and the Escuela Memory, started in Barcelona in 1994 by Àngels Gonyalons and Reguant. The director

---

[63] Roger, '*West Side Story*', pp. 1, 24; 'Publicidad USA', p. 19.

[64] Reguant, '1996 *West Side Story*' [online].   [65] Pérez de Olaguer, 'Llega un potente', p. 61.

[66] Subirana, 'Sueños de candilejas', p. 58.

acknowledged that many actors hired for *West Side Story* came from his school.[67]

The cast mostly included novice artists, besides veteran actors Pep Torrens and Enric Casamitjana in the adult roles of Schrank and Doc/Glad Hand, respectively. The press focused on two renowned artists: Víctor Ullate Roche as Bernardo and Alba Quezada as Maria. Ullate, son of famous dancers Víctor Ullate and Carmen Roche, had started his career in dance, but since attending the Rudra Bejart School in Lausanne (Switzerland) he also had longed to sing and act. The dancer acknowledged the difficulty of finding the proper training in Spain, where 'there's no school that teaches the three fields, singing, dancing and acting, at the same time'.[68] His participation in *West Side Story* began a remarkable career in musical theatre. Opera singer Alba Quezada, an American of Guatemalan descent, already boasted of wide experience in musicals, including in the original Broadway production of *The Phantom of the Opera*. She had also previously performed the role of Maria at the University of Southern California.[69] Quezada was 38 years old, although a reporter from *El Periódico de Catalunya* claimed that 'she doesn't look this age at all'.[70] The role of Tony went to Jordi Fusalba, an actor with experience in musicals, but he had to leave the production during previews because of vocal problems. His replacement was Lorenzo Moncloa, a zarzuela tenor who performed in the Spanish production of *Les Misérables* in 1992. Marta Ribera received the role of Anita, and Fedor de Pablos was Riff.

The premiere of *West Side Story* raised high expectations. Even though the 1983 and 1988 touring productions left no lasting influence in Spain,[71] *West Side Story* sporadically remained in the news in 1996. In the spring, students from the American School of Madrid had performed it in the school's gym.[72] During the summer, music from *West Side Story* again reached the mainstream Spanish media from the Olympic Games in Atlanta. The Spanish rhythmic gymnastics team won the gold medal after a performance with music that combined 'America' with 'I Got Rhythm' and 'Embraceable You' by George and Ira Gershwin; Spanish reporters only mentioned the reference to *West Side Story*.[73]

Reguant defined *West Side Story* as 'the father of all musicals';[74] according to Jordi Fusalba, 'this work is known by all kinds of people aged between 10 and

[67] Zorrilla, 'Hay Poca Atención', p. 76.   [68] Palomar, 'Víctor Ullate Roda', pp. 110–11.

[69] San Agustín, 'Alba Quezada', p. 9.   [70] Pérez de Olaguer, 'Cita de amor', p. 33.

[71] Pérez de Olaguer claimed that 'Never before had the musical created by Jerome Robbins been on a Spanish stage'. ('Cita de amor', p. 32.)

[72] Pérez de Pablos, 'Me gusta', p. 68.

[73] See, for example: Rullán, 'Las españolas', p. 36; Burgueño, 'Gimnasia dorada', p. 9; Winkels, 'España baila', p. 26; Roba and Arroyo, 'Madrid se llenó', p. 8.

[74] Salgueiro, 'Las bandas', p. 4.

70. It's a very current soap opera', and performing it for a musical theatre actor is the equivalent 'for an opera singer to do Tosca'.[75] When Reguant's touring production reached the Canary Islands, reporter José Orive reviewed the history of the American musical and of *West Side Story*, noting that experiencing such a relevant work was 'historical': 'It will be the first time for us to watch a spectacle of this kind.'[76] Given the show's themes, several artists and critics offered that the work was not outdated: a reporter from *Diario 16* stated that 'the New York West Side could easily be some cities south of Madrid. And their guys the new skins opposite to the immigrants in Fuenlabrada or Móstoles.'[77] Alba Quezada agreed:

> The reference to Shakespeare's *Romeo and Juliet* is universal and eternal. The idea of a love that is made impossible due to the pressure of the world that surrounds its protagonists is always current. As for the street violence, the confrontation between gangs or the prominence of one against the other is, sadly, a topical issue.[78]

Focus's production stood out as a major economic effort in an industry that was optimistic about its future in Spain, especially in the two country's main hubs for musical theatre: Barcelona and Madrid. Pérez de Olaguer noticed that 'Barcelona is today a city to consider when talking about musicals. Whether large or small in format, their presence in the list of available productions is now a regular fact.'[79] The press identified Reguant's initiative as a particularly large undertaking for the Spanish theatrical industry, with an emphasis on the unusually high number of live performing artists (33 actors and 22 musicians[80]) as well as the economic investment, which reached 211 million *pesetas* (approx. €1,268,000),[81] 'the most expensive show produced by a private company' to that date in Spain.[82] The investment quickly bore fruit: two days before the first preview performance they had already sold more than 16,000 tickets.[83]

Rehearsals started at the beginning of October 1996 at the cultural complex Tecla Sala in the city of L'Hospitalet,[84] lasting for two intense months. Alba Quezada made an interesting observation regarding the rehearsals: 'There, in

---

[75] Ginart, 'Pobres emigrantes', p. 19.   [76] Orive, '*West Side Story*', p. 20.

[77] Centeno, 'Aquel Barrio', p. 51.   [78] Pérez de Olaguer, 'Cita de amor', p. 33.

[79] Pérez de Olaguer, 'Cita de amor', p. 33.

[80] The Barcelona reviews stated that there were 22 musicians; the Madrid reviews reported 25.

[81] Though the number varies greatly among sources, the information provided by Pérez de Olaguer seems reliable. He breaks down the total of 211 million pesetas into three parts: 66 million for production, 98 million for operating costs, and 47 million for publicity. (Pérez de Olaguer, 'Llega un potente', p. 61).

[82] Muñoz-Rojas, '*West Side Story*', p. 7.   [83] Pérez de Olaguer, 'Cita de amor', p. 32.

[84] Vendrell, 'Los Sharks', p. 56.

the United States, everything's more rigid, there's less margin for improvisation. Here you work for more hours but, I'd say, with less concentration.'[85] Performances of *West Side Story* in Barcelona took place in the Tívoli, a 1,643-seat theatre owned by Pedro Balañá, the same entrepreneur that 34 years before had opened his Cine Aribau with the film of *West Side Story*. Preview performances started on 4 December, and the official premiere, scheduled for the 10th, was delayed until the 16th to facilitate the late incorporation of Lorenzo Moncloa as Tony. *West Side Story* remained at the Tívoli for five months, until 18 May 1997, one of Barcelona's most significant shows of the season,[86] before commencing with a national tour.

Between July and December 1997, the tour reached Gijón (Teatro Jovellanos), Santiago de Compostela (outdoors in the Plaza de la Quintana on 27 July), San Sebastián (Teatro Victoria Eugenia), Las Palmas de Gran Canaria (Teatro Pérez Galdós, as part of the 2nd Autumn Festival of Theatre and Dance), Figueres (Teatre Jardí), Murcia (Auditorio), Vitoria-Gasteiz (Teatro Principal Antzokia), Zaragoza (Auditorio de Zaragoza), Bilbao (Teatro Arriaga), Sabadell (Teatre la Faràndula), and Reus (Teatre Fortuny). The production settled in the Teatro Nuevo Apolo in Madrid from 16 December to 18 March 1998. They continued through Alicante (Teatro Principal), Palma de Mallorca (Auditorium), Valencia (Teatre Romà), Córdoba (Gran Teatro), Santander (Palacio de Festivales), El Ejido (Teatro Municipal), and Tarragona (Camp de Mart), finishing with two performances in Ibiza (Can Ventosa) on 18–19 July. Each stop included between one and eight performances, with the exception of Bilbao (15 performances), Valencia (17 performances), and of course Madrid. The production ran for 184 performances in Barcelona (131,526 spectators), 92 performances in Madrid (47,334 spectators), and a total of 97 for the remainder of the tour (64,272 spectators).[87] In a period of a year and seven months, Focus offered a grand total of 373 performances seen by more than 243,000 people.[88]

Throughout its two-and-a-half-month run in Madrid, *West Side Story* shared the spotlight with other prominent productions of American musicals: *El Hombre de la Mancha* (*Man of la Mancha*, Teatro Lope de Vega), *Sweeney Todd* (Teatro Albéniz, a rendition in *castellano* after the successful *català* version in 1995 at Barcelona's Teatro Poliorama), and *Los Fantástikos* (*The Fantasticks*, Teatro San Pol).

[85] Pérez de Olaguer, 'Cita de amor', p. 33.

[86] It was the show with the largest audience in Barcelona during the first trimester of 1997 ('Crece el número', p. 50.)

[87] Not counting the performance in Santiago de Compostela, for which we have no data.

[88] Information provided to the authors by Focus in February 2021.

Figure 3 Cover of the program for performances in the Teatro Nuevo Apolo (Madrid).

The confluence of these productions marked the beginning of an especially prolific period for the Anglo-American musical in Spain.

Taking advantage of the tour's sponsorship by Renfe (the country's principal railroad concern), the company of *West Side Story* travelled by train and offered short, promotional performances at some railway stations. This strategy was repeated in Gijón, Santiago, San Sebastián, and Madrid.[89] Some aspects of the production underwent important changes during the tour. Alba Quezada had left the company, Muntsa Rius (later replaced by Alicia Ferrer) and Virginia Martínez assumed the role of Maria. Paco Arrojo joined the cast to share the role of Tony with Lorenzo Moncloa. For reasons of economy, the producers substituted a recording for the orchestra, except in Madrid, where they hired the Iberarte Música ensemble.[90] The unfortunate lack of an orchestra would become a common practice in Spanish productions. The sets also had to be adapted to the possibilities of each stage. Some of these changes had a negative impact on the critical reception, as we will see later.

Adaptation

Reguant's adaptation was consistent with the position occupied by *West Side Story* in the collective Spanish memory: although two touring international productions had reached Spain, the work's indisputable reference was still the 1961 film. The director expressed his clear preference for the cinematic version, declaring that 'the characters from the movie are richer than the same ones in the theatrical original',[91] and even that 'the original text has many incongruities. In this sense, the movie is much brighter.'[92] The director therefore took the film as his main inspiration, while also considering the original text; he stated: 'The *West Side Story* in the Tívoli is much closer to the film than to the theatrical work. The staging follows basically the film and curiously we've performed some scenes of the original work that are not in Wise's film.'[93] This had important consequences at a structural level: the songs 'Cool' and 'Gee, Officer Krupke' exchanged places; 'America' landed before the Balcony Scene; and 'I Feel Pretty' moved to the beginning of the scene that leads to 'One Hand, One Heart'. In this last scene, Mas-Griera deleted Maria and Tony playing with mannequins, pretending they are their parents. The production added a brief reprise of the 'Mambo' at the start of the 'America' scene, with some Sharks dancing while Bernardo, Maria, and Anita present a dialogue added in the film. Also, in 'Somewhere', the nightmare sequence was cut.

---

[89] Gea, 'Estación Broadway', pp. 1, 4–5; Salgueiro, 'Las bandas', p. 4; C. T.: 'Más de treinta', p. 36; Pascual, 'Baile de bandas', p. 1.

[90] Duran, 'La América', p. 53.   [91] Pérez de Olaguer, 'Cita de amor', p. 32.

[92] '*West Side Story* llega', p. 24.   [93] Pérez de Olaguer, 'Cita de amor', p. 32.

Another significant change in Focus's production is placing the intermission just before the rumble, instead of after it, as in the original work.[94] This division, together with the redistribution of songs, established a notable distinction between the acts, where the work's most optimistic numbers happen in the first act and the most tragic ones (including the rumble and all the deaths) in the second. Reguant explains that 'I preferred the cinematic version because I thought it had more logic and preserved the idea of having fun before the deaths and tragedy just after them'.[95] The 'Tonight Quintet' was effective as a spectacular closing number for the first act.

The initiative of incorporating the cinematic modifications into the theatrical production caused a dispute with the rights holders, as Reguant explained:

> [I]t seems that Jerome Robbins found out about the changes and wanted to forbid the performances. We sent each other faxes and hundreds of phone calls, until fortunately Alba Quezada's husband interceded on our behalf with the choreographer's agent explaining the reasons for the changes. Our argument was that the Spanish spectator knew 'only' the cinematic version and would have believed that we had ourselves made the changes moved by a desire for notoriety and they wouldn't have understood them.[96]

Even though the film was their main reference, that did not prevent them from making creative decisions that went beyond that model, as Reguant comments concerning the work around Tony's character: '[W]e wanted a Tony that was different from the film, less sugary, cute, and snobbish. Tony is the hardest and more mature of the characters, a leader and ex-convict.'[97] He explains also that 'we've placed much more importance on the song "Somewhere", which is the one that carries the common thread of the second part'.[98] This idea led to an important modification in the second act's closing scene. After Maria has said 'Te adoro, Antonio', the last line in the original version, they added a full reprise of 'Somewhere', first sung by Maria as she urges Chino and Action to approach Tony's body, and then by the whole ensemble, before some of the boys lift his body and leave in procession. The rest leave in succession, accompanied by underscoring, until only a Shark, a Jet, and Angelito (Baby John) remain on stage. The first two seem ready to start a fight, but Angelito stops them with a gesture and they leave peacefully, his arms on their shoulders. This image mimics the conclusion of the ballet 'Somewhere', once more referencing this song's message of peace and finishing the work on a hopeful note.

---

[94] This decision was not motivated by the cinematic version, which offered yet another different point for an intermission, between the gang's war council and 'I Feel Pretty'.

[95] Reguant, '1996 *West Side Story*', [online].   [96] Reguant, '1996 *West Side Story*', [online].

[97] Gea, 'Estación Broadway', p. 5.   [98] '*West Side Story*, una historia', p. 72.

The choreography and orchestral arrangements had to be adapted to the limited possibilities offered by the Spanish theatrical industry at the time. As McNabb explained: 'I've tried to adapt Jerome Robbins's style, which is very singular, to the possibilities of the dancers and actors I've worked with.'[99] Concerning the orchestral arrangements, Emilio Solla (understudy conductor and pianist) asserted that 'Bernstein's scores, with the last arrangements he made, have been respected to the maximum',[100] but Miquel Ortega acknowledged that they had to manage without some of the reeds: '[H]ere we have the problem that the figure of the multi-instrumentalist, who plays nearly ten instruments, is very rare.'[101] The orchestration detailed in the Madrid playbill included four violins, four cellos, double bass, two clarinets, two saxophones, three trumpets, two trombones, guitar, drums, percussion, synthesiser, and piano. The musical director took pride in the work they did with the voices: 'We have achieved the contrast that Bernstein wanted between the more trained voices and the secondary ones.'[102] In any case, it was a complex task to achieve a balance among the cast's diverse vocal styles. A good example is Lorenzo Moncloa, whose training as a zarzuela singer might have had an undesired effect in his performance, as can be deduced from a negative review mentioned below.

Joaquim Roy designed a minimalistic set that provided a harsh urban atmosphere, with dark silhouettes of buildings in the background, combined with moving panels and an elevated walkway to provide a second level when needed, such as for the balcony scene. The indoor locations included simple elements: a counter and a panel with backlit windows for the bridal shop, a wall, and some lamps for the gym. The scenes in Doc's store and Maria's room occurred just outside these places, highlighting the dominant street ambiance. Props were reduced to the indispensable – Maria's dress in her first scene, a couple of chairs and a table in the war council, the rumble's knives, Chino's gun – enhancing the feeling of bareness.

Reguant assigned the text's adaptation to Albert Mas-Griera, a noted Catalan writer, translator, and screenwriter who had worked with the director on other occasions. He already had adapted to *català* such musicals as *Blood Brothers, Blues in the Night*, and *The Rocky Horror Show*; after *West Side Story* he would make other important contributions with adaptations to *castellano* of *Chicago, Mamma Mia!, Grease*, and *Les Misérables*.

For *West Side Story*, Mas-Griera worked first on an adaptation to *català*, since the original plan was to use this language, as had been done in Focus's previous

---

[99] Bravo, 'Focus sube', *ABC*, p. 93.   [100] Gea, 'Estación Broadway', p. 5.

[101] '*West Side Story*, una historia ', p. 72.   [102] Pérez de Olaguer, 'Cita de amor', p. 32.

productions. The difficulty of assembling a competent cast led to reconsideration, since it implied that the actors not only had to master the dancing, singing, and acting, but also speak this language. On the first day of auditions, they considered that the Puerto Rican characters might speak in *castellano* among themselves.[103] A production where *català* replaced English as the common language and *castellano* remained as the mark of the 'outsiders' would have been intriguing in Spain, where *castellano* is the common language and *català* spoken in the eastern autonomous communities. The latter plays a key role in the construction of cultural identity and in politics of independence. Ultimately, they decided to render the entire adaptation in *castellano*, resolving the problem of those who could not speak *català* and simplifying marketing the show outside of Catalonia. Reguant mentions that 'at some moment we considered the possibility of moving the action to Spain, but the music and the ambiance are difficult to relocate'.[104] When the decision to adapt to *castellano* was made, Mas-Griera already had a 'rather advanced Catalan version, which was completed with satisfactory results'. Referring to this and his later adaptation in *castellano*, he claims that 'both versions stand among the best – and most difficult – adaptations I've made'.[105] His rendition of *West Side Story* is faithful to the original text in meaning and tonal variety, alternating between vulgar street language and the poetry of lovers. In the sung text, the word's stresses maintain their correspondence with the music's accents, and most of the rhymes have also been preserved. We offer a detailed analysis of this production's text adaptation in Section 6.

Critical Reception

The critical reception of Reguant's production was generally positive but includes unfavourable comments. Some critics highlighted the show's world-class quality, as did Joan-Anton Benach in *La Vanguardia*: 'The music sounds like never before, as like never before the choreography presents a quality, rigour and pedigree from the USA that wasn't reached in any of the previous musicals produced by Focus.'[106] Referring to performances in Madrid, Lorenzo López Sancho from the daily *ABC* detected 'A warm performance, full of sincerity. ... Everything sounds good: the orchestra, the characters, on this stage organised on two different levels that facilitates the ensemble's movements.'[107] Enrique Centeno declared in *Diario 16* that 'this is a terrific spectacle, a musical of extraordinary quality in its orchestration, Castilian

---

[103] Subirana, 'Sueños de candilejas', p. 58.   [104] Gea, 'Estación Broadway', p. 5.
[105] Mas-Griera, email interview with the authors, September 2021.
[106] Benach, '¡Danzad', p. 54.   [107] López Sancho, '*West Side Story*, un musical', p. 97.

version (by Albert Mas-Griera), choreography and spectacle, that director Reguant has succeeded in preserving with all the magic of Broadway's original'.[108] The film's popularity contributed to a good audience reception, although was also a cause for comparison, like one made by Eduardo Haro for *El País*: 'the production doesn't reach ... the quality of the film everyone has seen, as the orchestra, which makes a serious effort, but doesn't have the quality of the symphonic orchestras that we have heard on recordings since that time'.[109]

The production's various creative elements received mixed reviews. Critics agreed that the best part of the show resided in McNabb's choreography. Julio Bravo commented in *ABC*:

> [McNabb] has realised a splendid and intelligent job (that would gain brilliance in a wider and more favourable stage than that of the Nuevo Apolo). Splendid because he knows how to make the most of the available human capital, doesn't make anyone dance above their possibilities, and manages the constant bursts of energy from the stage. And intelligent because he knows how to forget the essential from Robbins – that is, he doesn't pretend to be him nor copying his steps – while remaining faithful to his spirit.[110]

María Araujo's costume designs received unanimous praise. López Sancho perceived 'a highly functional set design, illuminated with current taste and really excessive in the use of shadows',[111] while Benach described the lighting as 'uneven' and 'disconcerting'.[112] Miquel Ortega's job directing the Taller de Músics orchestra in Barcelona inspired mixed commentary: while Joan Anton Cararach (*El Periódico de Catalunya*) stated that 'The orchestra is not superb, but has a very high level and, above all, is theatrical',[113] Mingus Formentor *(La Vanguardia)* gave a 'barely pass' to the performance of the demanding and iconic score.[114]

The textual adaptation was mostly praised. Cararach stated that 'the careful Castilian translation by Albert Mas-Griera is not the panacea for musical's lovers – that is, the original language –, but neither is it one of those so often sad Catalan versions that impoverish the most intelligent pieces of North American theatre'.[115] José Orive confirmed the merit of Mas-Griera's work:

> This version of *West Side Story* is rather accomplished musically and with a text that fits well, without letting the idioms used and language adaptations fall apart. To adapt Sondheim's lyrics without losing the original essence seemed an impossible task. Here they have achieved it, to the point one

---

[108] Centeno, 'Aquel Barrio', p. 51.   [109] Haro Tecglen, 'Odiosa comparación', p. 38.
[110] Bravo, 'Fieles al espíritu', p. 97.   [111] López Sancho, '*West Side Story*', p. 97.
[112] Benach, "¡Danzad', p. 54.   [113] Cararach, 'Apuesta', p. 57.
[114] Formentor, 'Peligros', p. 54.   [115] Cararach, 'Apuesta', p. 57.

forgets the known texts in English . . .. The musicality and the social commentary remain intact.[116]

A particularly negative review by Marc Sabater in the *Diari de Sabadell*, after one of the performances in this city near Barcelona, suggests that the show had suffered a loss of quality on tour. While acknowledging only the value of the choreography, he declared that 'the version we had the chance to watch in Sabadell borders on the pathetic. Because one can't give another rating to the image of a conductor with a baton in one hand and the compact disc controls in another, or to a patched and aesthetically ugly set, or to unspeakable lighting without disrespecting their authors.'[117]

Regarding the cast, several reviewers identified acting as the production's weakest point. Gonzalo Pérez de Olaguer stated in *El Periódico de Catalunya* that '[The audience] overlooks the deficient performance apparent in the scenes (mainly the dramatic ones) with only [spoken] text. The cast is one of dancers and singers more than of text actors.'[118] For his part, Benach declared that 'the purely textual parts are neither fish nor fowl. They are something blurry. . . . [W]ith a couple of exceptions in the first part, [spoken sections] fluctuate between naturalism and timid choral recitation.'[119] Nonetheless, performances of the main actors did not disappoint. Most reviews extol the merits of Lorenzo Moncloa (Tony) and Alba Quezada (Maria) and highlight the work of Marta Ribera (Anita) and Víctor Ullate (Bernardo). Pérez de Olaguer explained that 'Tenor Lorenzo Moncloa makes a very effective Tony, with a splendid voice that imposes itself at every moment. Beside him Alba Quezada exhibits her soprano voice with great authority and struggles to maintain an image of a *young girl à la Natalie Wood* that is perhaps not so achieved, but rather accepted by the audience.'[120] Cararach made some interesting observations about the style of both performers:

> [Alba Quezada] knows her character perfectly, presenting a María of high quality, but it is very probable that she will improve day by day: Quezada has in her head the *Maria* without accent, the María in English, and one can still notice small distortions in the vocal line of her character, derived from the change of language. . . . Something similar happens to Lorenzo Moncloa, Tony, because he incorporates in his role some slight zarzuela touches. In both cases they are, nevertheless, very minor details.[121]

In the abovementioned review by Marc Sabater, the reporter commented that 'the soloists seem to have been extracted from *La verbena de la paloma*'

---

[116] Orive, 'Un musical', p. 18.   [117] Sabater, 'A la ratlla,' p. 48.
[118] Pérez de Olaguer, 'Reencuentro', p. 61.   [119] Benach, '¡Danzad', p. 54.
[120] Pérez de Olaguer, 'Reencuentro', p. 61.   [121] Cararach, 'Apuesta', p. 57.

(a noted zarzuela),[122] a perception that perhaps was caused by those zarzuela style features detected in Moncloa's performance.

Ribera and Ullate received the most positive reviews. For Cararach, 'We are surprised by a very young Marta Ribera, a sensual, outsized Anita, that grows constantly and easily withstands the weight of two voices like those of Quezada and Lorenzo Moncloa.'[123] Benach compared their splendid work with the lead actors:

> There are obvious difficulties in an audition to find those who can sing, dance and deliver the text with absolute propriety. As the best common denominator of these disciplines stands, as I see it, Víctor Ullate Roche, a highly-trained dancer that also gets on very well in the face to face, and Marta Ribera, a very powerful woman in her dancing and talking that makes for a shameless and confident Anita. And there are two very worthy 'stars,' but with a narrower performative spectrum. ... They are Alba Quezada, a Maria of sweet gesture, voice and dance, and Lorenzo Moncloa, a Tony that brings great knowledge and professionalism to his singing.[124]

The audience confirmed these remarks in the performances in Gijón, as J. C. Gea narrated in the daily *La Nueva España*:

> As already happened in the cinematic version, the characters Anita and Bernardo – Marta Ribera and Víctor Ullate – raised the volume of the applause and caused a torrent of 'bravos'. The might of the junior Ullate beating with strength the Cuban-heel ankle spat [a reference to his exceptional dancing] and the joint work of Marta Ribera, an Anita as powerful as the libretto requires, earned unconditional fans.[125]

The production earned six nominations in the first two presentations of the Premios Max de las Artes Escénicas (1998 and 1999), the main national performing arts awards at that time: Best Musical Theatre Show in both presentations Best Costume Designer (María Araujo), Best Male Dance Performer (Víctor Ullate), Best Musical Director (Miquel Ortega), and Best Private Entrepreneur or Producer of Performing Arts (Focus S.A.).

The reaction from critics shows that Focus's production proceeded in a dignified but not infallible manner, operating in a demanding context where the criteria for quality had been hardened by the growth of productions of Anglo-American musical theatre in the country. The bar was set higher when it came to a show like *West Side Story*, which had been revered in Spanish culture for decades.

---

[122] Sabater, 'A la ratlla', p. 48.   [123] Cararach, 'Apuesta', p. 57.
[124] Benach, '¡Danzad', p. 54.   [125] Gea, 'Gijón', p. 3.

4 The *West Side Story* Summer Tour (2009)

A major presence in the *West Side Story* universe since 2000 have been productions of the show choreographed and directed by Joey McKneely and conducted by Donald Chan. McKneely is a Broadway dancer and choreographer who appeared in *Jerome Robbins' Broadway* (1989–90), where he learned some of the *West Side Story* choreography from Robbins himself. McKneely has also choreographed on Broadway, including the 2009 production of *West Side Story* directed by Arthur Laurents. Donald Chan, for more than the last thirty years the Bernstein Office's favoured conductor for the show, has directed *West Side Story* over 3,000 times all over the world.[126] McKneely and Chan teamed up in July 2000 for a production at the Teatro alla Scala in Milan, the first musical ever to play at the famed opera house. The show ran there again in July 2003, and since that time McKneely and Chan have led an intermittent world tour. Chan has stated: 'Joey and I always are trying to break the mould by casting young and talented performers.'[127] The tour came to Spain for visits to three cities during summer 2009: Madrid, 25 June to 5 July; Santander, 22 to 24 August; and Gijón, 26 to 27 August. The tour that summer was announced as a fiftieth anniversary celebration of the show's premiere on Broadway, misleading given its opening in September 1957. There are various accounts as to where else the tour played in 2009, one mentioning stops that included Sadler's Wells in London, the Chatelet in Paris, in addition to venues in Japan, Israel, Holland, Belgium, Switzerland, and Germany.[128] Another source states that the production also visited Beijing.[129]

In addition to leadership from McKneely and Chan, the production included set designs by Paul Gallis, costumes by Renate Schmitzer, and lighting by Peter Halbsgut. The producers were Michael Brenner for BB Productions GmbH with Sundance Productions and Juanjo Seoane Producciones. They double cast the two main roles, with Chad Hilligus and Scott Sussman appearing as Tony and Ali Ewoldt and Kendall Kelly as Maria. Other principals included Oneika Phillips as Anita, Emmanuel de Jesús Silva as Bernardo, and Michael Jablonski as Riff. McKneely and Chan chose a young cast, reportedly between 17 and 30 years old,[130] but it included major talents. Ali Ewoldt, for example, later played Maria in the American national tour based upon the 2009 Broadway version.[131] As stated by Julio Bravo in the Madrid daily *ABC*: 'Their intention is to recreate as faithfully as possible the original production, although, according to what McKneely told *ABC*, "the set design, costume, lights, and the style of

---

[126] Eslake, 'Donald Chan'.   [127] Eslake, 'Donald Chan'.   [128] Bravo, 'Broadway', p. 63.
[129] Figaredo, 'Amores', p. 64.   [130] Alvarado, '*West Side*', pp. M2, 8.
[131] Santamaría and Martínez, *Desde* Al Sur del Pacífico, vol. 3, p. 1299.

interpretation have been modified to make one forget the stereotypical image of the mounting in 1957"'.[132] Journalists variously reported the size of the company, including cast, technical staff, and musicians, as between 80 and 110 people, including 26 musicians in the orchestra, mostly members of the Symphony Orchestra of Lithuania with some players from the United States.[133] This was an expensive production and, as is clear from the media coverage, it was a challenge in the three Spanish cities to fund the effort. The company performs in English with supertitles in the language of their hosts. A survey of the production's reception in each city demonstrates that some members of the Spanish media were knowledgeable about *West Side Story*, including the stage version, and that they frankly evaluated the production. The show drew full houses in Santander and Gijón, displaying Spanish interest in the genre, interesting counterpoint to what Aurora Intxausti wrote in the Madrid daily *El País*. While introducing *West Side Story*, she noted that the musical is 'a genre that in Spain has not really taken hold'.[134]

West Side Story played in Madrid in the Casa de Campo, a large park on the city's west side, at a new outdoor venue, the Puerta del Ángel, with a seating capacity of 2,500.[135] The set included two metal structures, made to resemble wood and covered with multiple staircases like New York fire escapes. There were also frequent projections of black-and-white photographs of New York City in the 1950s. The show's local producer was the Ayuntamiento de Madrid, which set the ticket prices between 20 and 40 euros and hoped to raise 350,000 euros to help finance the visit. The series of performances was part of the summer program, 'Veranos de la Villa'. Writers in the Madrid media extolled *West Side Story*'s virtues in their preview articles, offering such lofty statements as 'its premiere [in New York in 1957] ... marked a before and an after in the development of the mostly genuinely American scenic arts'.[136] They also spoke of the 1961 film and described how the stage version is different. Julio Bravo of *ABC* praises director McKneely for 'this dazzling and emotional mounting, an example of quality and high artistry'. Although he finds the costumes 'excessively gaudy', he appreciates 'A magnificent show that you will enjoy from the rise of the curtain'.[137] Miguel Ayanz, writing in *La Razón*, enjoys that the show was in English, lamenting, '[W]hat mania it is to destroy such musical beauties by translating them'. He takes issue with those who complained that the

---

[132] Bravo, 'Broadway', p. 63.

[133] Bravo, 'Broadway', p. 63. Bravo reports that the musicians are members of the 'Orquesta Sinfónica de Lituania', perhaps meaning what is now called the Lithuanian National Symphony Orchestra.

[134] Intxausti, 'El musical', p. 82.   [135] Marinero, 'Romeo', p. 41.   [136] Marinero, 'Romeo'.

[137] Bravo, 'El genuino sabor'.

production included nothing original or risky, noting that the audience needs to realise how innovative the show was in its own time, also offering that he witnessed 'a great night of theatre' presented by 'great artists'.[138]

The company left Spain for Japan before returning in the last third of August to play in Santander and Gijón. In Santander, capital of the autonomous community of Cantabria, *West Side Story* was part of the Festival Internacional de Santander, playing four performances in the Sala Argenta del Palacio de Festivales; a Sunday matinee was added when three performances sold out. The fourth offering also sold out, meaning that 6,000 people saw *West Side Story* in Santander. Ricardo Hontañón, writing in *El Diario Montañés*, calls the production one of the festival's 'struts',[139] and Santander's mayor, Javier López Marcano, considered it a 'milestone' for his city to host the tour, hoping that it would be a significant addition to their application for the title 'European Cultural Capital' for 2016. Those in the media introducing the show presented interesting perspectives on its history and its music. Roberto Blanco, for example, writing in *El Diario Montañés* includes numerous details in his preview article and places *West Side Story* above competing realizations of *Romeo and Juliet* by such composers as Bellini, Gounod, Berlioz, and Prokofiev.[140] In his review in *Mundo Clásico*, Blanco laments the production's 'absence of more originality, risk' and the 'gaudy and simpleton' costumes 'like those in a bad … film about Hispanics and Yankees'. He thinks the orchestra 'sounded good' although with 'some maladjustment between brass and strings', and the amplified voices 'lost freshness and naturalness'. His opinions of the principals are mixed, but he notes that Oneika Phillips 'dazzled as a brilliant Anita.'[141] Laura Mier, writing in *Alerta*, finds that 'the show functions and continues delighting our senses thanks to a dramatic discourse that does not falter but grows the full length of its two hours of duration, and a choreographic and musical conception of such quality that it sustains itself'.[142]

Two days later, on August 26, the touring company opened in Gijón (Asturias) for two performances. The visit was partly made possible by support from the Fundación Cristina Masaveu Peterson. The run sold out at the Teatro de la Laboral, which accommodates an audience of 1,300. As reported in the news media, many of the city's leading citizens attended.[143] Gijón was unable to add another performance, as had been done in Santander. Its run was part of a brief summer season that also included two of Puccini's operas. The company usually spent two days setting their show up in the theatre, forcing them to work through the night.[144] Press coverage of the Gijón run engendered a fascinating

---

[138] Ayanz, 'Todo'.   [139] Hontañón, 'Vigor', p. 68.   [140] Blanco, 'Tony', p. 73.
[141] Blanco, 'Bodas'.   [142] Mier, 'Aún y siempre', p. 56.   [143] 'Primeros espadas', p. 62.
[144] 'Broadway llega', p. 1.

reaction from Carlos José Martínez, writing for *La Nueva España*. He opens his review by stating that he bought a *West Side Story* score while on a trip to the United States, and that he attended the show 'Score in hand', especially enjoying the 'Balcony Scene', 'Cool', 'I Feel Pretty', and the 'Somewhere' sequence. He approves of all five principals, describing their voices and performances in some detail. Martínez praises the show for its profundity, placing it among the finest works of musical theatre. For Martínez, the major difference between the 1957 stage version and the film is in the orchestrations, offering that the former is 'in fidelity with the aesthetic and academic tendencies of the same composer'. Martínez also states that the Spanish audience can come closer to the show's original spirit by hearing it in English. He declares: 'Adaptation, never translation.'[145] The controversy continues, however, and nine years after this manifesto, SOM Produce chose to produce *West Side Story* in *castellano*, a production considered in the next section.

5 'El clásico original de Broadway ... ' (2018)

Introduction

The centenary of Leonard Bernstein's birth came in 2018, sparking commemorations all over the world, a number of them involving *West Side Story*. SOM Produce, a major producer of musical theatre in Madrid, announced a mounting of the show for fall as part of the celebration. Their marketing slogan, 'el clásico original de Broadway', meant that they planned the first Spanish production based upon the original 1957 version in New York and not the 1961 film, which had been the case with Ricard Reguant's 1997 production. This meant, among other things, that musical numbers would be presented in the order of the original show. As has been the case with several efforts launched by these producers since the company's founding in 2010, their version of *West Side Story* found considerable success in its run of more than seven months in Madrid and ten months of touring around Spain before being closed by the COVID-19 pandemic in late winter 2020. The show opened in Madrid at an auspicious time for its musical theatre industry. Five major productions premiered that fall: *West Side Story, Anastasia*, and *El jovencito Frankenstein* (*Young Frankenstein*), each adapted from the American originals; along with *33* (on the life of Christ) and *El Médico* (based on the novel *The Physician* by Noah Gordon), both works by Spanish writers. In addition, *Billy Elliot* was in its second season and *El Rey León* (*The Lion King*), its eighth.

---

[145] Martínez, 'Un clásico', pp. 1–2.

The company's name, SOM Produce, derives from an abbreviation of the English title of their first show, *The Sound of Music*, known as *Sonrisas y lágrimas* in Spanish. Their offices are on Madrid's Gran Vía – a wide street in the centre of the city on which one finds several of the main theatres – near the famous Plaza de España. The company administers four of the city's main theatres: the Rialto, Calderón, Apolo, and Nuevo Alcalá. They schedule their shows in the capital city in these venues and also run tours. Anglo-American musicals that the company (and its predecessor) have produced in Spain have included, among others: *Avenue Q*; *Billy Elliot*; *Cabaret*; *La Cage aux Folles*; *Chicago*; *Fame*; *Grease*; *High School Musical*; *Jesus Christ Superstar*; *Mamma Mia!*; *Priscilla, Queen of the Desert*; *Saturday Night Fever*; *The Sound of Music*; and *We Will Rock You*. José María Cámara, (who died in 2021) was one of the firm's five partners. He described SOM Produce as a 'small business', held privately in two different companies, each owning 50 per cent of SOM stock. He lamented: 'We haven't anyone behind us, just our pockets!'[146] SOM Produce has demonstrated a knack for offering intelligent, marketable adaptations of Anglo-American shows, an excellent example being *Billy Elliot*, which ran at the Teatro Nuevo Alcalá from 2017 until being shut down by COVID-19 in March 2020. The rendition boasted an excellent translation/adaptation into *castellano* by David Serrano, a first-class production, and fine cast. Serrano, a leading Spanish director of films and stage productions, also directed the show. The authors will be providing, in this section, their own commentary on this production because they were able to see it.

The Adaptation/Translation of *West Side Story*

SOM Produce's first task for *West Side Story* was to secure a fresh translation/adaptation of the book and lyrics, a project accepted by Serrano. He adapts lyrics with his brother Alejandro, a musician, who helps ensure that textual accents fit the pre-existing music. The details of Serrano's adaptation will be approached in the next section; here will be a description of his general approach.

Serrano reports that he introduces fewer changes in a book adaptation that he prepares for another director, and for *West Side Story* he wrote for director/choreographer Federico Barrios.[147] Serrano wanted to ensure that his lyrics and dialogue 'sound good in *castellano*' while using phrases that did not seem too old or too modern and recognising that the show's characters 'are people of the

---

[146] Personal interview with José María Cámara (interview by P. R. Laird and G. Fernández Monte, Madrid, Spain, 3 January 2019).

[147] The quotations and paraphrased statements come from a personal interview with David Serrano (interview by P. R. Laird and G. Fernández Monte, Madrid, Spain, 6 January 2019).

Figure 4 Cover of the program for SOM's production of *West Side Story.*

street'. In general, Serrano sought a more natural discourse than did Albert Mas-Griera in the 1996 version, where dialogue between Tony and Maria tended to be more poetic. Serrano hopes that his adaptation sounds like a show originally written in *castellano*, a high bar indeed. He changed emphases in the book that he found 'quite weak . . . quite loose'; Serrano describes some of the characters as 'fools', pointing especially to Baby John, whom he tried to make less superficial. Serrano wanted to render Maria as 'more mature than she is usually portrayed'. Serrano said that he could not make his adaptation a hundred per cent faithful to the original because 'the humour is different; the language is distinct'.

Serrano felt humbled preparing translations of songs from *West Side Story* because he considers them some of the genre's finest. Along with his brother, they tried to ensure that their textual accents fit with the music like those of Sondheim. The Serrano brothers also observed Sondheim's rhymes and use of assonance and consonance, trying to make their work sound close to the original English. For example, in 'I Feel Pretty', where Sondheim placed 'charming' or 'alarming' in four consecutive, short lines, Serrano came up with 'Soy brillante/ Deslumbrante/Fascinante/Radiante/Lo sé' (I am brilliant/Dazzling/Fascinating/ Radiant/I know'). Serrano altered images and phrases that carry no useful meaning in *castellano*. A major problem is that there are many more monosyllabic words in English; Serrano has a list of every monosyllabic word in *castellano* and notes: 'With five syllables in English one can say a great deal; in Spanish it is very difficult to say anything in five syllables.' Serrano found love songs the most problematic, including 'Maria', 'Tonight', and especially, 'Somewhere'. Serrano is 'very proud' of what they accomplished with other songs, including, for example, 'Gee, Officer Krupke', 'America', 'I Feel Pretty', 'Cool', and 'Something's Coming'. Serrano found working on 'Krupke' to be 'fun'. His efforts pleased the work's licensers at Music Theatre International, which has made his adaptation available in Spanish-speaking countries.

The Director/Choreographer and Production

Federico Barrios is an Argentinian director/choreographer who previously performed these functions for SOM Produce in their 2015 production of *Cabaret*. He has trained in New York City at the Actor's Studio and in Molloy College's summer musical theatre program, Collaborative Arts Project 21. He discovered his career watching the films of *West Side Story* and *The Sound of Music* as a boy and found his mature inspiration to work on the former show in 2010 when he saw the Broadway production directed by Arthur Laurents. When SOM asked Barrios to direct the show, he states: 'I felt like they had put the world in my hands'.[148] His preparation was arduous: one year studying book and score in English and then months with Serrano's translation and adaptation. Given the need to reproduce Jerome Robbins's choreography, Barrios began with the 'bible' one receives from Music Theatre International,

---

[148] "Carta del Director," p. 5.

which explains what dancers do on each beat of the music. Barrios had it rendered in Spanish, assisting the translator with choreographic terms.[149] He studied the source for three months and consulted videos for more clarity; the guide states, for example, in what direction to thrust an arm, but not how far. His watchlist included the 2009 Broadway production, *West Side Story* segments in *Jerome Robbins' Broadway*, and other sources. Barrios concluded that he could not reproduce all of Robbins's work, mixing what he knew with recreations. (See Figures 5 and 6 for classic poses from Robbins's choreography that Barrios rendered with his cast.) Once he had a cast, he informed them: 'It is not simply dancing. It is dancing and all day telling the story.'

Figure 5 The Sharks dance during the 'Prologue' in SOM's production. (Photo by Javier Naval, in public domain.)

---

[149] The quotations and paraphrased statements come from a personal interview with Federico Barrios (interview by P. R. Laird and G. Fernández Monte, Madrid, Spain, 4 January 2019).

Figure 6 The Jets dance during the 'Jet Song' in SOM's production. (Photo by Javier Naval, in public domain.)

Barrios termed the audition process 'very hard'. There were 3,000 aspirants, including performers from Italy, France, and Portugal, but they had to able to speak Spanish without an accent. Auditions consumed a month – six days per week, six hours per day. Successful cast members went through five phases, each time performing a different song with choreography, and also performed four scenes. Relying on stereotypes, those cast with darker complexions became Sharks while the fairer actors became Jets. The cast tended to know *West Side Story* from the film, which meant that their work required careful study of the differences in the stage production.

The director's interpretation started with the show's famous songs and choreography, which he calls 'classics', aligning himself with SOM Produce's advertising line. Barrios found the show's major challenge to be telling the story without distracting from the music and dances. Their eight weeks of rehearsals started on 26 June 2018, nearly the same day (24 June) that Robbins commenced his rehearsal period of the same length with the original cast in 1957.[150] Barrios began with a workshop on *Romeo and Juliet* and proceeded to the musical, lecturing and analysing each scene before

---

[150] Simeone, *Leonard Bernstein*, p. 48.

working them. Only later did he add music. He enumerated which scenes he considers the most difficult: when Tony guiltily enters Maria's bedroom and she pardons him, with much occurring during this 'very short' scene; 'Gee, Officer Krupke', full of tension but also entertaining, confusing Spanish audiences expecting 'Cool' at this point from their knowledge of the film; when the Jets taunt Anita and rape her in the drugstore, a very powerful moment in SOM's production; and the final scene, which Barrios changed by deleting the procession and leaving the tableau on stage with the show's title descending in large letters from the fly-space. He added some of his own touches, such as Bernardo hiding a gun at the beginning of the show so that the audience later sees Chino retrieving it before he goes after Tony. A challenge for the choreography was the Teatro Calderón's small stage, especially during the 'Mambo' and 'Somewhere'. The latter number did not include the 'Nightmare', which Barrios likes, but he thinks the show is too long and the producers also wanted that sequence cut.

Barrios changed David Serrano's 'very good' adaptation in places during rehearsals, for example restoring some of Maria's lines in the 'Meeting Scene' that the adaptor had cut and adding lines for Anita in her animated discussion with Bernardo before 'America' in reaction to the '#MeToo' spirit. Although Serrano had added profanity, Barrios introduced more in rehearsals because he found its effect 'economic' (a powerful addition while using few words), appreciated how it complemented the music's strong rhythms, and mimicked the speech one hears in Madrid's *barrios*.

Barrios supervised the show's designers: the set by Ricardo Sánchez Cuerda, lighting by Carlos Torrijos and Juan Gómez Cornejo, sound by Gaston Briski, and costumes by Antonio Belart (design) and Ana Llena (production). Barrios started to work with his design team one year in advance with extensive discussions, seeking agreement on how to proceed before such debates delayed progress on the show. Barrios notes that it was 'a very long process but ... marvelous'. Barrios avers that his design team was not influenced by the original production: 'Everything is original to here.' When showing off set designs during our interview, the director commented on representing the fire escape outside of Maria's bedroom, pointing out 'the balcony with the moon', the most striking part of an otherwise realistic set design, with a large, blue, crescent moon (see Figure 7) combined with an image of more tenements. Barrios noted that the costume designs for females in the cast were influenced by the film's bright, bold colours.

The cast was strong and distinctive. Javier Ariano and Talía del Val starred as Tony and Maria. Del Val, who previously had played Belle in *Beauty and the Beast*, Cosette in *Les Misérables*, and Christine in *Phantom of the Opera*, has the stronger

Figure 7 The 'Balcony Scene' in SOM's production with the blue moon over Maria's bedroom. Javier Ariano as Tony and Talía del Val as Maria. (Photo by Javier Naval, in public domain.)

voice with a clear, powerful high range. Ariano, who worked with the Madrid-based La Joven Compañía, was convincing in his role and sings in more of a pop style. About once per week, their fine substitutes were Jan Forrellat and Ana San Martín. Silvia Álvarez, who has appeared in numerous musicals in Madrid, is a lithe, stylish dancer who sings and acts well and made for a memorable Anita, bringing real pathos to the taunting scene. Bernardo was played nobly by Oriol Anglada, and Víctor González was a virile Riff who sang well.

In Madrid, an orchestra of eighteen musicians accompanied from the tiny pit with brass above and behind the set. The music director was Argentinian Gaby Goldman, who has led the music in more than ninety productions.[151] The orchestration was: piano, keyboard, three violins, cello, bass, four reeds, bassoon, two trumpets, horn, trombone, drums, and percussion. Except for the lack of a guitar, this corresponds with one of Music Theatre International's (MTI's) approved orchestrations for the show.[152] The orchestra provided a vital presence in the cozy Teatro Calderón, if with small issues of intonation and ensemble.

---

[151] The Stage Company, 'Gaby Goldman', http://thestagecompany.com.ar/gaby-goldman/.
[152] www.mtishows.com/west-side-story.

The Producer's Angle

In an interview from early January 2019, a few months after *West Side Story* opened at the Teatro Calderón, José María Cámara, one of five producers of SOM Produce, spoke of the show's reception, plans for its future, and its place in the Spanish musical theatre market. He reported that the rendition was appreciated and selling well, especially among older people, which did not surprise Cámara, who often found that the average age of the audience is not unlike that of the age of the play, and *West Side Story* is over 60 years old. He did not expect young people to attend it and saw no reason to market it to them, grateful that in Madrid 'we have a lot ... of old people with good health and money and time to go' and see *West Side Story*.[153] Complaints from audience members that Cámara had heard included the show's length, the knife fight during the rumble and the 'very dramatic' second act, and differences between the stage version and the 1961 film.

SOM Produce plans its advertising carefully: they spend no money on print ads in favour of signs on buses and in the Metro, use of the internet and radio, and publicity from interviews and television appearances by cast members and those on the creative staff. SOM finds that Madrid's theatre audience mostly helps to fill the seats during a run's first season, after which they require more of the tourist trade, a reason for the industry's hard push to tout the city as a major centre for the genre.

West Side Story ran in Madrid at the Teatro Calderón (see Figure 8) from 3 October 2018 until 2 June 2019,[154] the title's longest run ever in Spain as a stage musical in a single venue. They ran eight shows per week, adding another around Christmas. SOM planned a lengthy tour that started in late June in the Canary Islands, necessitating that the scenery be placed aboard a ship. Planned later stops included about two months in Barcelona, several weeks in Valencia and Bilbao, and about one week or less in numerous other cities. A problem was the size of the pits in some theatres, which would not accommodate the 18-piece orchestra used in Madrid; Cámara stated that they were in discussions with MTI about possible solutions. The tour was interrupted on 14 March 2020 by the pandemic.[155]

Besides admissions, other revenue lines from the show for SOM Produce were limited. They sold playbills and souvenirs, but only the former and the less expensive souvenirs sold well. Cámara reported that there was more money to

---

[153] The quotations and paraphrased statements come from the abovementioned personal interview with José María Cámara.

[154] González, '*WEST SIDE STORY*'. According to this article, the tour would play in the following cities: Las Palmas, Santa Cruz de Tenerife, Málaga, Bilbao, Salamanca, Valladolid, Alicante, Zaragoza, Mallorca, Jérez, Murcia, Vigo, Gijón, Sevilla, Barcelona, Pamplona, Santander, Cádiz, San Sebastián, Logroño, Sant Cugat, Córdoba, Valencia, and Vitoria.

[155] www.westsidestory.es/

Figure 8 The Teatro Calderón, on the Calle de Atocha, where SOM's production played in Madrid. (Photo by Paul R. Laird.)

be made from the theatre's bar than the souvenir stand, and they did not sell souvenirs on tour. Columbia Pictures made a special DVD version of the 1961 film to sell in conjunction with the SOM production, but few were purchased.

Critical Reception

SOM Produce's rendition of *West Side Story* was a distinctive critical success in Madrid. Of the nineteen reviews from print and web sources consulted, thirteen were raves, five positives, and only one mixed. One reason for this overwhelmingly positive response was the show's overall quality, but one also detects cheerleading from critics pleased to see that the city's musical theatre industry's ability to present this challenging show. As Estrella Savirón writes on *agolpedeefecto*, 'Undoubtedly, it is a difficult and valiant assignment to adapt such an emblematic work, that survives in the collective imagination of various generations'.[156] Aldo Ruiz of *El Teatrero* is even more specific about possible difficulties and stating the production's basic success:

> It is not easy to bring to the stage a musical of the size of *West Side Story* because it has been done in so many versions, including the famous film, that always runs the risk – inevitable, on the other hand – to fall into dreaded comparisons. SOM Produce – responsible, among others, for *Billy Elliot, el Musical* – has been responsible for facing head-on this great challenge, producing a new adaptation. And, for us, the result is more than notable.[157]

Nacho Fresno of *Shangay* writes with outright boosterism: 'It is not an easy assignment to stage *West Side Story*. And if it can be done today with success in Madrid it is thanks to the very high level that we have in this country to present shows like this.'[158] It is hard to imagine a similar note being struck by a reviewer in New York or London.

Several of the writers wanted readers to understand the show's place in the genre's history and reputations of its creators. The anonymous writer for *PaseandoaMissCultura*, for example, offers:

> From the first note to the last sign, *West Side Story* is one of the most important and representative musicals in the universal theatre. The score by Leonard Bernstein and Stephen Sondheim is unanimously known as one of the best in the history of musicals, the text by Arthur Laurents continues to be so touching and real as on the first day and the original choreography of Jerome Robbins occupies a place of honour in the story of contemporary dance. In his hands, the greatest story of love took to the streets of Broadway to be converted into one of the milestones of musical theatre in every age.[159]

Such praise of the property is not unusual in these reviews.

David Serrano's adaptation received almost universal approbation, even if his contribution was often missed by critics. Estrella Savirón allows that his version in *castellano* 'permits that both the lyrics of the songs and the dialogues do not seem forced and maintain a vocal coherence'.[160] Horacio Otheguy Riveira of *Culturamas* offers that Serrano 'prepared a very careful translation into *castellano* and adapted the text so that the rhythm never flags'.[161]

Numerous critics praised the director. For example, Otheguy notes: 'The main person responsible for the great quality of this *West Side Story* ... is Federico Barrios, director and choreographer, who achieved a magnetic staging

---

[156] Savirón, '*West Side Story*'.   [157] Ruiz, '*West Side Story*'.   [158] Fresno, 'Crítica'.
[159] 'Opinión de *West Side Story* El Musical'.   [160] Savirón, '*West Side Story*'.
[161] Otheguy, '*West Side Story*'.

in a show closest to ballet and to opera, but with the dynamism of rock opera and touches of jazz.'[162] Ruiz finds that Barrio's work was assisted by the set:

> Federico Barrios has done an excellent job as director of the production and adaptor of the original choreography of Jerome Robbins. Betting entirely on classicism, Barrios offers us a magnificent staging sustained by spectacular scenography – designed by Ricardo Sánchez Cuerda – that combines the classic and elegant tone, with other more modern elements . . .[163]

Raquel Vidales of *ElPais* describes the scenery as 'striking and suggestive' but wonders if Sánchez Cuerda might have been thinking of a larger stage because when 'many dancers participate; they seem squeezed together'.[164] Andrea Mori of *OKDiario* praises the set design as 'brilliant', if also 'a set of the old type, with few technological elements. The story does not need them.'[165] Concerning costuming by Antonio Belart (design) and Ana Llena (production), Lidia Nieto praises their 'great work' that, along with the staging, 'almost through art performed the magic of traveling to New York in the fifties'.[166] A reviewer for *TopCultural* lauds the 'colourful costumes' in terms of how they complemented the choreography and 'in the end evoke, along with the chiaroscuro lighting, the film from 1961 directed by Jerome Robbins and Robert Wise'.[167] As noted above, this resemblance of the costuming to the film, especially for the women, was intentional for Barrios. The colourful costumes provided an important element in a production where much of the set, besides the extravagant blue moon, bore the muted colours of tenements and a highway overpass. Otheguy was one of several critics who found the lighting effective, stating: 'Carlos Torrijos and Juan Gómez Cornejo have composed a very rich lighting scheme, with many hues, that functions like a musical score, creating its own symphony'.[168]

Positive feedback from critics continued concerning the music. A recurring theme in the reviews was surprise and praise for the live orchestra, which is not a given in Spanish musical theatre. Shows have been done in Madrid with recorded accompaniment, and sometimes ones that have a live orchestra while running in the capital city dismiss musicians before the subsequent tour and then work with recordings. Ricardo Castillejo, writing a brief review for *Sevilla Magazine*, includes a note of surprise about the live orchestra in his overall praise for the production: 'A marvelous mounting, faithful to the original and the film, in which everything functions to perfection – from the lighting to, why not, the sound of live orchestra'.[169] The anonymous reviewer from

---

[162] Otheguy, '*West Side Story*'.   [163] Ruiz, '*West Side Story*'.   [164] Vidales, 'El Bernstein'.
[165] Mori, '#PlanesLook'.   [166] Nieto, '*West Side Story*'.   [167] '*West Side Story* como nunca'.
[168] Otheguy, '*West Side Story*'.   [169] Castillejo, 'El amor'.

PaseandoaMissCultura also praises the 'live' band.[170] Aldo Ruiz gives the orchestra and music director strong praise: 'Magical numbers would not be possible without the marvelous orchestra with Gaby Goldman at the head during these first days. An enormous pleasure to be able to enjoy these legendary songs by Bernstein with this exquisite director.'[171] Most reviewers were also impressed with the voices in the cast. Otheguy, for example, reminds his readers of 'the high level of musical difficulty for the actors' but 'the majority of the dancers sing ... with beautiful solo voices'.[172] The unnamed critic for *TopCultural* thinks that those casting the show might have 'opted for more personality in some of the principal voices'.[173]

Most reviewers complemented what they saw as a strong cast. Aldo Ruiz, for example, states: 'A fantastic group of actors and dancers, very homogeneous that, of course, forms one of the bulwarks in that which sustains this mounting of *West Side Story*'.[174] Estrella Savirón notes the cast's abilities as triple-threats: 'The entire cast realises a committed and very worthy effort; the quality of the dances, the acting, and the vocal is evident.'[175] Raquel Vidales was less impressed with the acting on opening night, praising the cast's work during the musical numbers but noting that they were less effective 'in the spoken scenes; very rigid in the first performance.'[176] An anonymous writer praises the cast's 'rapport during the musical numbers and including during the discussions',[177] perhaps reference to the believable reactions one saw on the faces of each actor throughout the show.

Javier Ariano and Talía del Val, playing the two lovers (see Figure 9), drew detailed attention from critics. Some descriptions of Ariano's work were ecstatic. Andreu Rami of *TeatroMadrid* offers: 'Javier Ariano, the young actor who plays Tony, is possibly the best actor in musicals that I have seen in my life. ... [H]e has a precious voice from which the text to the music jumps out with such truth and naturalness that you cannot help being carried away by the story.'[178] Aldo Ruiz was clearly impressed by the young actor, lauding his 'notable characterisation' and 'precious voice, controlled with sensitivity', but also noting that he had less experience than some of the other members of the cast and would improve during the run.[179] The more experienced Talía del Val was a darling for the majority of reviewers, especially for her voice, described as 'incredible' and 'prodigious'.[180] Duets by the lovers sparked some

---

[170] 'Opinión de *West Side Story* El Musical'.   [171] Ruiz, '*West Side Story*'.
[172] Otheguy, '*West Side Story*'.   [173] '*West Side Story* como nunca'.
[174] Ruiz, '*West Side Story*'.   [175] Savirón, '*West Side Story*'.   [176] Vidales, 'El Bernstein'.
[177] 'Opinión de *West Side Story* El Musical'.   [178] Rami, 'Mejor imposible'.
[179] Ruiz, '*West Side Story*'.
[180] 'Opinión de *West Side Story* El Musical'; Ruiz, '*West Side Story*'.

Figure 9 Javier Ariano as Tony and Talía del Val as Maria singing 'Balcony Scene' in SOM's production. (Photo by Javier Naval, in public domain.)

disagreement. Ruiz terms their joint numbers 'particularly beautiful and delivered with magic and a great deal of chemistry'.[181] Vidales finds it 'jarring' that they sang 'in distinct styles: her, lyrical; him, more melodic'.[182] 'Lyrical' would seem to mean that del Val has a voice that one can imagine in an operetta while Ariano's voice is more popular in sound. The juxtaposition was noticeable and at times distracting.

Silvia Álvarez was a strong Anita (see Figure 10). Juan Bravo of *ABC* calls her 'the highlight above all' among the actors, with 'the heart-rending spirit and sensuality necessary for the character'.[183] Otheguy memorably states: 'The vitality with which this *barcelonesa* imbues the character splatters the walls of the Calderón, despite being shaken once and again by the cruel prejudices and rancidness of both gangs.' He finds her character's journey 'one of the most beautiful narrative arcs of this dizzying story'.[184] The reviewers had less to say about Oriol Anglada as Bernardo and Víctor González as Riff, but Aldo Ruiz describes the former as '[w]ell applauded' and the latter as 'impeccable in each of the disciplines that an actor in musicals ought to excel'.

---

[181] Ruiz, '*West Side Story*'.   [182] Vidales, 'El Bernstein'.   [183] Bravo, 'Respetuoso'.
[184] Otheguy, '*West Side Story*'.

Figure 10 Silvia Álvarez as Anita and Oriol Anglada as Bernardo in 'The Dance at the Gym' in SOM's production. (Photo by Javier Naval, in public domain.)

The production won two awards in the twelfth presentation of the Premios Teatro Musical, the main prizes that have been granted to Spanish musical theatre productions since 2007: Best Choreography (Federico Barrios and Jerome Robbins) and Best Sound Design (Gaston Briski). In the BroadwayWorld Spain Audience Awards 2019, the production won the awards for Best Touring Musical and for Best Choreography.

More than one of the Madrid critics noted the timeless quality of *West Side Story* as a version of *Romeo and Juliet* and as a work that transcends its own period. Andreu Rami tied the story to the issue of immigration, which could hardly have been more current throughout the world when the show opened in 2018:

> *West Side Story* was written in 1957 based on *Romeo and Juliet* by William Shakespeare (1597), but it continues to be more current than ever. Centered on the problems derived from Latin American immigration to the United States, one must be grateful to reopen the debate to approach the theme of immigration in an epoch when politicians respond with wild, racist speeches about the exodus of victims of wars in our neighbouring countries. Maria and Tony make it clear for us: more discussion, more love, and more peace.

The great irony in the United States is that Puerto Ricans do not need to immigrate to the United States. They are already citizens, free to move elsewhere if they wish. Yet for many Americans they remain part of the Hispanic 'Other' coming from south of the border.

West Side Story as a Classic in Interpretation and Reality

There are many questions to ask when reviving a show from another period. Does it still have something to say in the modern world? Are there segments that cannot successfully be presented today? Will the styles of the music and choreography resonate with modern audiences? Will the show be understood in terms of its intentions and provide entertainment value? The situation is complicated when a translation/adaptation is required because the show will be presented in an entirely different culture. SOM Produce decided that *West Side Story* still had something to say and produced a rendition, except for the extensive use of strong language, that would have been recognisable to audiences from the late 1950s. David Serrano rendered the show's book as comprehensible and relevant to a modern, Spanish-speaking audience, and the lyrics he produced with his brother Alejandro Serrano are singable and carry the necessary aesthetic punch. Along with director/choreographer Federico Barrios, SOM Produce declared Bernstein's music and Robbins's choreography to be classics, worthy of faithful reproduction in a different culture more than six decades after the show's premiere. The show's commercial and critical reception indicates that SOM Produce won their bet, but they could have approached the show very differently.

Critic Aldo Ruiz stated the possibility in his review: 'There will always be voices that ask that when a major revision of this classic, why not make it an adaptation for our time, the year 2018?'[185] He goes on to allow that Serrano could have performed this task as well, arriving at another updated version of the classic story. Indeed, Ivo van Hove's new Broadway production of *West Side Story*, which suffered the misfortune of opening just three weeks before the COVID-19 shutdown in March 2020, was a substantial rethinking of the show, including new choreography. However, SOM Produce planned its revival for a country where the original stage version was not well known; the story, Robbins's choreography, and Bernstein's music were famous from the film. Placing these familiar elements into the context of a traditional staged version was a major contribution to the Spanish audience's knowledge of this iconic show and a useful step in the popularisation of Anglo-American musical theatre in Spain. Re-interpretations of *West Side Story* and other classics from its time will remain frequent throughout the world in the years to come, but Spain probably needed to see the show in more or less its established form before

---

[185] Ruiz, '*West Side Story*'.

a director, for example, places the story in a totally different setting with a different artistic approach.

6 Comparing the Spanish Adaptations by Albert Mas-Griera (1996) and David Serrano (2018)

In this section we analyse the Spanish adaptations of *West Side Story* by Albert Mas-Griera (1996) and David Serrano (2018), comparing each with the show's original text, to appreciate how varied approaches and criteria bring about different results. We worked with unpublished documents of the texts kindly provided by Ricard Reguant and SOM Produce, and a recording of a performance of Focus's production at the Teatre Tívoli.[186]

In both versions, the adaptors reduced the size of the ensemble by deleting secondary members of each gang. Mas-Griera replaced all of the characters' nicknames formed with English words with Spanish ones: Action became *Acción* (literal translation), A-Rab was *Nervio* ('nerve', 'vigour'), Baby John was *Angelito* ('little angel'), Snowboy was *Colilla* ('cigarette butt'), Big Deal was *Cuatrojos* ('four-eyes'), Anybodys was *Inútil* ('useless'), and Glad Hand was *Besugo* (colloquially 'dumb'). Serrano also changed the name of numerous minor characters.[187] Among the more famous of the Jets, Action, A-Rab, and Diesel became *Jack*, *Ian*, and *Mike*, respectively. Among the Jets girls, Anybody's became *Pauline*, but she wants to be called *Paul* and become part of the gang. In Laurents's original, some of the Sharks have English nicknames (e.g., Anxious, Nibbles, Moose); these characters were cut in both adaptations. The names of principals and adults did not change. In Mas-Griera's version, Tony's given name, Anton, turned into *Antonio*, much more common in Spain, as had already been done in the dubbing of the 1961 film; Serrano restored the original name with a Spanish pronunciation: Antón. The name of the Sharks, translated to Tiburones in the movie's dubbing, remained in its original English form in both theatrical adaptations.

Structural changes made in Reguant's version, mostly related to their reliance on the film as a model, were explained in Section 3. In contrast, there are no structural changes compared with the original work in SOM's adaptation, intended to be based on the Broadway original. One exception, like the

---

[186] A. Mas-Griera, [adaptor], *West Side Story*. [hereafter identified as 'Mas-Griera']. D. Serrano, [adaptor], *West Side Story* [hereafter identified as 'Serrano']. Ricard Reguant: *WEST SIDE STORY (1er acto)*. www.youtube.com/watch?v=nDZJZWTwi-w. Ricard Reguant: *WEST SIDE STORY (2° acto)*. www.youtube.com/watch?v=VGe-R6M0ri8. Comparisons with the book and lyrics of the original production were realised from: Shakespeare, *Romeo and Juliet* and Laurents, Bernstein, Sondheim, and Robbins, *West Side Story* [hereafter identified as 'Laurents/Sondheim'].

[187] Serrano.

Barcelona rendition, was cutting the nightmare section of the 'Somewhere' ballet, a common deletion.

The Book

Concerning the adaptation of spoken dialogue, both Mas-Griera and Serrano were faithful to the original text in style and meaning, but details reveal important differences in approach. Generally, one observes that Mas-Griera strived towards a literal translation, while Serrano chose to sacrifice literal meaning in favour of a text that sounded natural in *castellano*.

Having taken the film as a reference, Mas-Griera modified some dialogues with ideas from equivalent moments in the screenplay. Some exact quotations from the film's Spanish dubbing in his adaptation suggest that at times he used that as his model rather than the film's original English dialogue. For example, the line 'And born like we was on the hot pavement', made by a Jet to Krupke in the film's first dialogue,[188] was adapted as 'You were born in the street too',[189] an inaccurate translation with the exact same words as in the film's Spanish dubbing. Aside from these conversations modified in the movie, Mas-Griera remained faithful to the original theatrical text. He claims: 'The cinematic version affected Reguant's decisions more than mine. . . . I remained as faithful as possible to the original musical – but an adaptor never has the last word on certain decisions, except when these really betray their work'.[190] Mas-Griera translated all stage instructions literally, and spoken dialogues follow the original with few minor alterations. None of these changes affect the plot, although some of them impact our perception of Tony and his relationship with Riff. For example, in the dialogue before the 'Jet Song', Cuatrojos (Big Deal) mentions that Tony 'Had been scared stiff when he spent five days in jail',[191] an explanation as to why he left the gang; also, in the first dialogue between Tony and Riff, Mas-Griera cut lines in which the latter states he has been staying with Tony's family to avoid living with his uncle.

The original text by Laurents and Sondheim includes several elements that pose major challenges for adaptation to another language: street slang, terms that denote nationality (often offensively), occasional Spanish words, and a poetic tone for Maria and Tony. Regarding street slang, both Mas-Griera and Serrano drew upon current colloquial expressions that match the speech of young Spaniards. One consequence of this in both adaptations became frequent use of profanity, which separates these adaptations from the original text and the

---

[188] This line came from a later scene of the original theatrical version (Laurents/Sondheim, p. 205).
[189] 'Eh, que usted también nació en la calle'. Mas-Griera, p. 3.
[190] Mas-Griera, email interview with the authors, September 2021.
[191] '¡Se le pusieron por corbata cuando estuvo cinco días en la cárcel!' Mas-Griera, p. 5.

film's script (original and dubbed); strong swearing would have been rare on the Broadway stage or in a Hollywood film from the period. In 1957, producers had not allowed Sondheim to use the word 'fuck' as the lyricist strived for a realistic portrait of the characters' manner of speaking, following the teachings of his mentor Oscar Hammerstein II.[192] The same caution appeared in the cinematic version and, of course, its Spanish dubbing, consistent with the strict censorship applied to everything during the Francoist era. This limitation no longer existed in the Spain of the 1990s, so Mas-Griera added realism by hardening expressions. So did Serrano 22 years later, though less often. An interesting example is Baby John's sexist insult to Anybodys, 'Ah, go walk the streets like ya sister',[193] translated in the Spanish dubbing of the movie 'Go fry asparagus, you dumb thing' (a bland and childish insult, but based on a common Spanish idiom), while Mas-Griera wrote 'You go home and learn to cook, you piece of shit!' Serrano returned to a literal translation of the original phrase.[194]

Mas-Griera use of profanity was striking. Shrank's threat to the Jets in their first dialogue, 'I'm gonna beat the crap outa everyone of ya', became 'I'm gonna fuck you alive.'[195] Action's 'Where the devil are they?' became 'Where the fuck are they?'[196] Bernardo's lines 'Let's get down to business' (in the war council) and 'Let's get at it' (in the rumble) were translated as 'Let's get to the fucking point' and 'Let's fucking start.'[197] The word 'guts', used by Bernardo and Tony in the rumble, became 'balls'.[198] Tony's desperate call to Chino 'Come get me, damn you!' became 'Come get me, you damn bastard!'[199] Interestingly, Riff and Tony's friendly motto 'Womb to tomb' was initially translated in Mas-Griera's adaptation as 'Cunt to tomb',[200] but the recording reveals that the word *coño* ('cunt') finally became *vientre* ('womb'). In a broad sense, Mas-Griera strove to exploit the verbal violence. In the overture, where the original stage instructions explain that the initial aggressions by gang members also feature 'overly elaborate apologies', the adaptor indicates instead 'all with an endless amount of profanity and insults'.[201]

---

[192] Furia and Lasser, *America's Songs*, p. 260.   [193] Laurents/Sondheim, p. 170.

[194] '¡Vete a freír espárragos, pedazo de boba!' (movie dubbing); '¡Tú vete a casa y aprende a cocinar ...! ¡Pedazo de mierda!', Mas-Griera, p. 19; 'Anda, vete a hacer la calle como tu hermana', Serrano, p. 43.

[195] Laurents/Sondheim, p. 139; 'Voy a joderos vivos', Mas-Griera, p. 3.

[196] Laurents/Sondheim, p. 169; '¿Dónde coño se han metido?', Mas-Griera, p. 19.

[197] Laurents/Sondheim, pp. 175, 190; 'Vayamos al grano de una puta vez', 'Empecemos de una puta vez', Mas-Griera, pp. 22, 32.

[198] Laurents/Sondheim, p. 191; 'cojones', Mas-Griera, p. 32.

[199] Laurents/Sondheim, p. 222; '¡Ven a por mí, maldito cabrón!', Mas-Griera, p. 44.

[200] 'Del coño a la tumba', Mas-Griera, pp. 6, 7, 30.

[201] Laurents/Sondheim, p. 138; 'Todo esto acompañado de un sinfín de palabras soeces e insultos', Mas-Griera, p. 2.

Another important set of decisions in the adapting process is how to deal with expressions related to nationality. In the movie's Spanish dubbing, the term 'American' had been translated as *norteamericano* ('North-American'), a proper rendition since in Spain the word *americano* includes people from the entire Western Hemisphere. Mas-Griera and Serrano, however, preferred to use *americano*, limiting the word's meaning to someone from the United States. In a related matter, both adaptors made a couple of interesting additions in the descriptions of Anita and Rosalia when these characters first appear. They specify that Anita's outfit is not only 'slightly flashy' but 'American',[202] displaying in advance her attitude towards acceptance of her new culture that she expresses in 'America'. In contrast, where the original instruction says Rosalia is 'more quietly dressed', Mas-Griera offers that she 'dressed in a Spanish manner', and Serrano writes 'with Hispanic tones'.[203]

In Mas-Griera's adaptation, Schrank and the Jets refer to the Sharks repeatedly with the word *latinos* ('Latins'), while Serrano wrote *sudacas* ('greasers'), the English translation being a common derogatory term for Latin Americans in the United States. In the war council scene, insults directed by Pepe and Indio towards the Jets, 'Micks' and 'Wop', were translated by Mas-Griera to 'Indians and Polacks'; Serrano used here 'shitty Irish' and 'spaghetti', preserving the specificity of the original insults to Irish and Italian people, respectively.[204] For the racist epithets that the Jets hurl at Anita in the taunting scene, 'Gold tooth', 'Pierced ear', 'Garlic mouth' and 'Spic! Lyin' Spic!,' Mas-Griera inserted greater verbal violence: 'Shitty gypsy', 'Black cunt', 'Dirty mouth', and even 'Go back to Puerto-Shit, you fucking liar.' Serrano's insults here, although a bit less violent, are still hurtful: 'You're only a bitch', 'You stink of garlic' and 'Shitty greaser'.[205]

In the original text, Laurents made clever use of some Spanish words, not only to emphasise cultural differences, but also to express Tony's sympathy for the Puerto Ricans after he falls in love with Maria. This strategy disappeared in both Spanish adaptations, where it seems impossible to imply when characters should be speaking in Spanish as opposed to the pretended (but non-existent) English. Mas-Griera underlined which words were in Spanish in the original,

[202] Laurents/Sondheim, p. 150. 'un vestido algo llamativo, "americano"', Mas-Griera, p. 8. 'un vestido estilo "americano" un tanto llamativo', Serrano, p. 22.

[203] Laurents/Sondheim, p. 164. 'vestida a la manera española, con tonos apagados', Mas-Griera, p. 13. 'discretamente vestida con tonos hispanos', Serrano, p. 37.

[204] Laurents/Sondheim, p. 176; 'indios', 'polacos', Mas-Griera, p. 23; 'irlandeses de mierda', 'espagueti', Serrano, p. 48.

[205] Laurent/Sondheim, pp. 218–19; 'Gitana de mierda', 'Coño negro', 'Boca sucia', 'Vuélvete a Puerto-Mierda, jodida mentirosa', Mas-Griera, p. 42; 'Solo eres una zorra', 'Apestas a ajo', 'Sudaca de mierda', Serrano, p. 93.

but in performance no distinction is possible. Neither of the Spanish productions made use of different accents to differentiate the nationalities of characters, which might have sounded artificial and was unnecessary to follow the
plot. Nevertheless, this led to a loss of certain interesting details from the
original English text. In the sixth scene, when Tony wishes Doc 'buenas noches,
señor' in Spanish, the old man instantly understands that Tony has fallen in love
with a Puerto Rican.[206] Serrano solved this by having Tony tell Doc that he has
been to the moon and 'a very special Puerto Rican girl lives there'.[207] In the next
scene, Tony greets Maria and Anita again with 'buenas noches'; Anita corrects
him: 'It's too early for *noches. Buenas tardes.*' Here, Mas-Griera provided
a direct translation of Anita's remark (comprehensible by an attentive spectator), while Serrano simply deleted it.[208] Interestingly, when Tony and Maria
declare their love to each other with 'te adoro' in the balcony scene, Serrano
inserted an additional line for Maria, 'Tony, te quiero', the standard form of 'I
love you' in Spain, where 'te adoro' sounds unnatural.[209]

Among decisions of a cultural nature, Mas-Griera's adaptation curiously
indicates that the Sharks leave Doc's after the war council (expelled by
Schrank) whistling Woody Guthrie's 'This Land is Your Land', instead of
'My Country, 'Tis of Thee', as indicated in the original version.[210] However,
as revealed in a video recording of the production, the Sharks whistled 'My
Country 'Tis of Thee', probably better known in Spain than Guthrie's song.

Regarding the poetic tone common in Tony and Maria's spoken lines and
songs, Mas-Griera and Serrano followed contrasting criteria, mainly in the
dialogue. The former prepared literal translations while the latter modified
the text that he thought sounded unnatural in Spanish. For example, consider
the scene when the lovers first meet: 'My hands are cold. Yours, too. So warm. /
Yours, too. / But of course. They are the same.' Mas-Griera adapted this literally
but included the line 'Your cheeks are burning', using a colloquial expression
that adds intensity; however, the idea that both pairs of cheeks and hands 'are
the same' sounds very strange in Spanish. Serrano deleted this last line about
similarity and made Maria simply answer, 'Yes'.[211] We find another example in
the lines 'I see you. / See only me', right before the 'Tonight' duet. Mas-Griera
again wrote a literal translation that sounds somewhat forced in Spanish.
Serrano, instead, replaced these lines with the phrase 'But they don't see you

---

[206] Laurents/Sondheim, p. 180.
[207] 'Que he ido a la luna y he vuelto. Y te voy a contar un secreto: en la luna vive una chica
puertorriqueña muy especial', Serrano, p. 52.
[208] Laurents/Sondheim, p. 181; Mas-Griera, p. 27; Serrano, p. 53.   [209] Serrano, p. 37.
[210] Mas-Griera, p. 24; Laurents/Sondheim, p. 179.
[211] Laurents/Sondheim, p. 155; 'Mis manos están frías. Las tuyas también. Tus mejillas queman. /
Las tuyas también. / Claro. Son las mismas', Mas-Griera, p. 11. Serrano, p. 28.

like I do', spoken by Maria, referencing the racial antagonism.[212] Given the poetic feeling of songs between the lovers, where literal translation is impossible because of limitations in the number of syllables, we find numerous creative choices in both adaptations, as will be explained below.

Details on Serrano's Version

Whereas the most important aspect of Mas-Griera's adaptation is his reliance on the film, one can better understand Serrano's rendition with a brief trip through it, showing its similarities and differences with the original Broadway version. The word 'translation' does not describe his work. Making the show immediately comprehensible in *castellano* necessitated judicious rewriting. In Act 1, Scene 1, for example, one notes his meticulous approach in describing the gang leaders. Whereas Laurents called Riff 'glowing, driving, intelligent, slightly whacky' and Bernardo 'handsome, proud, fluid, a chip on his sardonic shoulder', Serrano's version varied, dubbing Riff a 'natural leader' and his counterpart 'spontaneous and with airs of superiority'.[213] The franker nature of Serrano's Spanish adaptation becomes apparent once dialogue starts after the 'Prologue'. Lt Schrank opens his harangue at the gangs with 'I don't give a shit'.[214] In the Jets conference that follows, Baby John's 'Gee', spoken in concern about the blood on Ian's pierced ear, becomes 'Fuck', an epithet he later repeats, fearing pistols mentioned as possible weapons in a rumble. As noted above, Mas-Griera also had made this choice.[215] Often Serrano deleted lines, such as shortening the Jets' discussion of Bernardo's piercing Ian's ear. Serrano also removed words played for double meanings in English that will not work in Spanish. Riff's speech before 'The Jet Song' again demonstrates Serrano's tough approach with references to 'this shit of police' and 'to fight against those pigs', referring to the Sharks.[216]

Scene 2, opening with Riff imploring Tony to come to the dance that evening, closely parallels the English version, but there are differences. Serrano, for example, makes no reference to 'sky-writing' to describe the sign that Tony is painting for Doc. Mas-Griera also had omitted this reference, consistent with the 1996 version's minimal staging where Tony is not painting a sign but simply moving soda crates. Returning to Serrano's adaptation, Scene 3 in the bridal

---

[212] Laurents/Sondheim, p. 161; 'Te veo a ti. / Solo a mí', Mas-Griera, p. 17; 'Pero ellos no te ven como te veo yo', Serrano, p. 34.

[213] Laurents/Sondheim, p. 137. 'líder por naturaleza', 'espontáneo y con aires de superioridad', Serrano, p. 9.

[214] 'Me importa una mierda que os matéis entre vosotros', Serrano, p. 10.

[215] Laurents/Sondheim, pp. 140, 142. 'Joder', Mas-Griera, 4. 'Joder', Serrano, pp. 11, 13.

[216] 'Pero con esta mierda de policías', '¡Tenemos que pelear contra esos cerdos, y enseñarles quién manda aquí!', Serrano, pp. 12–13.

shop includes a few differences as Anita and Maria argue over lowering the neckline of the latter's dress for the dance before Bernardo and Chino arrive, but the essential meaning remains the same. Serrano handled the dance at the gym in Scene 4 with responsible changes to clarify meanings, such as deleting reference to the 'settlement house' in the stage directions and changing description of the dancing.[217] The nervous emcee, Glad Hand, in the original only tries to laugh at the slur on his sexuality, but in Serrano's version he explains himself with 'I always like there to be a bit of humour.'[218] Serrano tried to pare down Maria's lines in the 'Meeting Scene', but director Federico Barrios needed more dialogue to accommodate Bernstein's underscoring. Serrano made no attempt to render Laurents's original slang in Spanish, substituting 'Obviously' for 'Right, Daddy-o.' Aggressive language directed towards opponents common in the Spanish version appears again towards the end of the scene when Riff says to Tony 'We're going to shatter these chickens' rather than the original 'Let's get the chicks [here meaning their girlfriends] and kick it'.[219]

The lengthy Scene 5 includes both the 'Balcony Scene' and 'America'. A major difference occurs as Tony leaves Maria. He does not tell her that his given name is Anton; rather, she states that the Puerto Rican version of Tony is 'Antón'. Then, later in the scene, Maria addresses him differently and says 'Tony, I love you'. Before 'America', when Bernardo and Anita argue about how different New York is than Puerto Rico, they are more confrontational than in the original. In Scene 6, at Doc's where the Jets await the Sharks' arrival for the war council, Serrano changed a number of lines and his frank approach reappears when Pauline answers Doc about her intended adult profession. Laurents wrote 'A telephone call girl', but Serrano baldly wrote: 'I am going to work having telephone sex.' Mas-Griera had gone further here by making Anybodys declare that 'I will be a luxury whore!'[220] In Serrano's adaptation, the women are more interesting in this scene than in the original, where they spout little more than meaningless jive. In the Spanish version, Graziella teases the boys about being afraid of what might happen in the rumble. Much of the scene's remainder proceeds predictably but with a harder edge and a considerable amount of profanity.[221]

In places, Serrano provides more explanation than one reads from Laurents. For example, after Anita leaves in Scene 7, Tony's optimistic 'Don't worry. She likes us!' becomes from Serrano 'It is very clear that to her we seem a good

---

[217] Serrano, p. 25.   [218] 'Me gusta que haya siempre un poquito de humor', Serrano, p. 26.

[219] Laurents/Sondheim, p. 157. 'Claro', 'Vamos a destrozar a esas gallinas', Serrano, p. 30.

[220] Laurents/Sondheim, p. 171; '¡Yo una puta de lujo!', Mas-Griera, p. 22; 'Yo voy a trabajar haciendo sexo telefónico', Serrano, p. 44.

[221] Serrano, p. 50.

couple'.[222] Dialogue between Tony and Maria before 'One Hand, One Heart' is much like the original. Scene 8, the 'Tonight Quintet', opens with similar stage instructions; the song will be covered below. In Scene 9, the rumble, Serrano again declined to find a Spanish equivalent of Laurents's slang words, like 'buddy boy',[223] and continued his wont in making the dialogue more confrontational. Also, in the *castellano* version, Bernardo makes no speech about the mutual hatred between the gangs, and Tony never calls Maria's brother 'Nardo', only to be corrected.[224] Later, Bernardo's taunting is more aggressive, with 'Are you chicken?' becoming 'You are a shit.'[225] He calls Tony a 'coward' and a 'shitty Polack'.[226] The stage instructions in Scene 9 are very similar in both versions.

Scene 1 in Act II includes 'I Feel Pretty', Chino and then Tony coming to Maria's bedroom, and the dream ballet with 'Somewhere'. There is little surprising in Serrano's version but a few subtle differences: Maria's friends are more sarcastic at the opening of the scene and with Maria during and after her opening song; in an added stage instruction, Chino calls to Maria off-stage before entering; Tony speaks more about going to the police before Maria convinces him not to; and there are a few subtle differences in stage instructions for the ballet. Barrios and SOM Produce insisted that the 'Nightmare' sequence be cut to shorten the show.

Scene 2 includes a scene between Baby John and Ian before Krupke enters. They escape from the policeman and encounter other Jets; the gang sings 'Gee, Officer Krupke' before Pauline enters and tells them that Chino has a gun and intends to kill Tony. Serrano prefers that 'Cool' be sung here, as in the film,[227] but SOM Produce purposefully did the stage version. Serrano again avoided rendering American slang and humour in *castellano*. Baby John's absurd line to Krupke, 'We got twenty-twenty hearing', became 'We are a little deaf'.[228] The scene ends with Pauline revelling in her opportunity to impress the gang with the way she gathered information, an exchange that continues to demonstrate Serrano's frequent use of profanity.

Scene 3 finds Tony and Maria together in her bed as Anita seeks comfort from her friend. When Tony discovers that Anita is outside the room, he reacts. Serrano gives Maria more nerve when she observes that now he is afraid. The remainder of the scene, involving 'Boy Like That/I Have a Love' and Schrank

---

222 Laurents/Sondheim, p. 182; 'Está clarísimo que le parecemos una buena pareja', Serrano, p. 54.
223 Laurents/Sondheim, p. 190; Serrano, p. 62.   224 Laurents/Sondheim, pp. 190–1.
225 Laurents/Sondheim, p. 192; 'Eres un mierda', Serrano, p. 63.
226 'Cobarde', 'Polaco de mierda', Serrano, pp. 63–4.
227 The quotations and paraphrased statements came from a personal interview with David Serrano.
228 Laurents/Sondheim, p. 204; 'Estamos un poco sordos', Serrano, p. 78.

questioning Maria, closely resembles the original. In Scene 4, Anita goes to Doc's with a message for Tony from Maria only to be taunted and assaulted by the Jets. Serrano cannot use the double meaning of 'pass' in English: in Laurents's version, Anita wishes to 'pass' to speak with Tony and the Jets answer that 'She's too dark to pass', meaning for a white person.[229] In *castellano*, the line becomes clearer for Spanish ears: 'I'm sorry. Passing is prohibited for girls with such dark skin.'[230] When Anita lies about Chino shooting Maria before leaving, Serrano has her add that Maria is dead. Scenes 5 and 6 in this adaptation are mostly similar to the English version, including the final procession, which Barrios eschewed in favour of a final tableau.

The Songs

Regarding the adaptation of sung text, Mas-Griera declared that the key word for this task is not so much 'translation' as 'transportation': 'I don't really think that translation is possible. We have to readjust, to relocate, to make people forget the original song, the original language, so they can read or listen with naturalness to what has been translated.' For him the song should 'sound like it isn't the translated version', and maintains that it is important to focus on preserving 'the cadence, the rhythm, ... the sense of poetry and music'.[231] Spanish adaptations have often failed to follow these rules, and 'many translators fall into the trap of crossing accents, contorting the language and abusing the classic Castilian hyperbaton when facing the English verse'.[232] Mas-Griera acknowledged the special difficulty in adapting materials by Bernstein and Sondheim: 'There's nothing easy in [these authors]. Sondheim – a superlative genius – is feared and admired, when someone's adapting him, both for his lyrics and his music'. He remembers 'Something's Coming' and 'I Feel Pretty' as 'tough nuts to crack', although 'difficulties arose everywhere' in the work, whose adaptation was 'a great challenge'. All in all, he claims that 'I think I got over the majority of obstacles'.

In Mas-Griera's adaptation, song lyrics seem to follow the same rules as those for spoken text, a search for literality while conforming to different tones of speech (i.e., colloquial, aggressive, poetic, etc.). Songs with more poetic content and form such as the 'Tonight' duet or 'Somewhere', where it was much harder to produce a literal translation, show more creative solutions, as we shall see.

---

[229] Laurents/Sondheim, p. 217.

[230] 'Lo siento. El paso está prohibido a las chicas con la piel tan oscura', Serrano, p. 92.

[231] 'ANOTACIONES', www.youtube.com/watch?v=Y5nS2chAHG8.

[232] Mas-Griera, email interview with the authors, September 2021. The remaining quotations from this paragraph are from the same interview.

Throughout the entire work, Mas-Griera excelled at preserving the placement of rhymes and matching textual and musical accents.

As noted above, Serrano felt humbled in preparing Spanish lyrics for *West Side Story* songs with his brother Alejandro. He states that he could take more license when rendering the lyrics for *Billy Elliot* in *castellano* – perhaps suggesting that the show simply does not have the same status in the repertory. He believes that literal translation usually is untenable because of the need for lyrics to fit Bernstein's music and different senses between the languages. For example, Serrano notes that 'I love you' is a strong statement in English, but he finds the corresponding 'Te quiero' in Spanish to be less so, so he used other phrases in his love songs. Serrano reports that they tried to pay attention to Sondheim's rhyme schemes and use of assonance and consonance; however, as will be seen, this was not always possible. Serrano wanted to ensure that his lyrics matched the sense of the dialogue, while also altering images or phrases that lack meaning in *castellano*. Serrano studied translations of lyrics into Spanish that Lin-Manuel Miranda did for the 2009 Broadway revival, including material for the Sharks in Spanish. Serrano considers Miranda 'a genius' but found problems in the American's work. For example, to open 'A Boy Like That', Miranda wrote 'Ese cabrón' ('That bastard'),[233] with an accent on the first syllable, unlike the English line 'A boy like that'. Serrano instead wrote 'El muy cabrón',[234] which adds 'very' for emphasis and also places accents on the second and fourth syllables, corresponding with Sondheim's line. 'El muy cabrón' is a phrase one will hear from Spaniards in moments of profound anger. Serrano continued to revisit his translations, looking for improvements. For example, Sondheim's 'I Feel Pretty' includes the notion that Maria should receive the 'key to the city', which Serrano used in the script from April 2018 consulted for this study,[235] but Spanish cities do not honour dignitaries in this fashion, so later Serrano deleted the idea. A step in finishing the project was showing the translations to Gaby Goldman, the production's musical director. The licenser of *West Side Story*, Music Theatre International, had right of refusal on Serrano's translations; he reports that they asked for four or five changes in his adaptation, which has now become the official version for the Spanish-speaking world. Our survey and description of songs in these two versions of *West Side Story* in *castellano* will help demonstrate Serrano's approach.

The 'Jet Song' in Sondheim's version describes the gang's camaraderie, one's status as a member of the group, and their physical prowess. Mas-Griera's version highlighted the gang's braggadocio and general hostility. The song

---

[233] *West Side Story: The New Broadway Cast Recording*, booklet, p. 31. It was for this production that Lin-Manuel Miranda wrote Spanish lyrics for several of the songs.

[234] Serrano, p. 87.   [235] Laurents/Sondheim, p. 196; Serrano, p. 69.

starts with the strong declaration that 'You are a Jet and a good Jet is a god.'[236] The tone becomes more aggressive in the last verse: 'Don't fuck with the Jets,/ Emigrate or die!'[237] The final lines add self-reflexive humour: 'You damn bastard,/What are you doing here?/Get out of our song!'[238] Focus's production included the verse in which the Jets sing about the dance at the gym, which appears neither on the 1957 Original Cast Recording nor the cinematic version. SOM omitted this section as well, part of their fidelity to the original production.

Serrano admitted that he somewhat changed the meaning of the 'Jet Song', emphasising the gang's potency and capacity to defeat the Sharks. The first verse, which Riff sings, only has one reference to the gang's cohesion ('And you will not be alone when [problems] come'[239]). In the verse that the Jets sing after Riff exits, they describe the Sharks as 'shit', and the final two images are of the Jets fighting 'with an animal instinct' and holding their opponents 'always under our feet'.[240]

For Tony's 'I want' song, 'Something's Coming', Mas-Griera was consistent with his adaptation of the title line as 'Ya se acerca' (literally 'It's coming'). Mas-Griera's and Serrano's adaptations of the first four lines of the song are identical: 'Quizás,/Tal vez,/Hay algo ahí,/Algo más' ('Perhaps,/Maybe,/There's something there,/Something more'). This and other similarities suggest that perhaps Serrano knew Mas-Griera's work. Serrano stuck to general phrases about waiting and finding satisfaction in what might arrive, mostly avoiding Sondheim's more concrete imagery (i.e., telephones, raps on doors), although this *castellano* version does include the line 'A light/A smell/A sound/Or her voice'.[241]

Mas-Griera's adaptation of 'Maria' provided beautiful lines that mention 'The sounds of God, of love, when I think of you', and claim that 'The name of heaven is Maria.'[242] For Sondheim's lines where Tony suggests the effects of uttering her name at various volumes, Mas-Griera wrote 'Say it loud and it burns your soul,/Say it soft and it fills you with calm.'[243] Serrano's realisation of 'Maria' is more comparable to Sondheim's original with emphasis on her name and the effect of hearing it, such as 'Shout it and it will fill your soul./Sing it and

---

[236] 'Eres un Jet y un buen Jet es un dios', Mas-Griera, p. 5.

[237] 'No jodáis a los Jets,/¡Emigrad o morid!', Mas-Griera, p. 6.

[238] 'Maldito cabrón,/¿Qué haces tú por aquí?/¡Sal de nuestra canción!', Mas-Griera, p. 6.

[239] 'Y no vas a estar tú solo cuando vengan [los problemas]', Serrano, p. 14.

[240] 'estas mierdas puertorriqueñas', 'pelear con instinto animal', '¡ . . . siempre bajo nuestros pies!', Serrano, p. 16.

[241] 'Una luz/Un olor/Un sonido/O su voz', Serrano, p. 21.

[242] 'Los sonidos de Dios, del amor, cuando pienso en ti', 'El nombre del cielo es María', Mas-Griera, p. 13.

[243] 'Dilo fuerte y te quema el alma,/Dilo flojo y te llena de calma', Mas-Griera, p. 13.

you will feel such calm.'[244] It is interesting to note the use of the rhyming words 'alma' ('soul') and 'calma' ('calm') in the same places Mas-Griera had used them. Serrano found the show's love songs to be the hardest to translate; his work on 'Maria' consumed weeks.

'Tonight', in both the 'Balcony Scene' and 'Quintet', features bold choices in each version. The duet is a song where Mas-Griera applied a creative adaptation where it seemed impossible to translate literally every idea. The opening line 'Tonight, tonight' was translated as 'Amor, amor'[245] ('love'), a choice already made by Augusto Algueró in his adaptation of this song in 1962, as mentioned in Section 1. The phrase meaning 'tonight' in *castellano*, 'esta noche', cannot work with Bernstein's music, although it sounds well in *català*, 'aquesta nit', (four syllables for the double 'tonight', with similar accents) as we already observed in Salvador Escamilla's version from 1963. Mas-Griera preserved the anaphora in Sondheim's three consecutive lines starting 'What you . . . ' with the text 'Quiero ver,/quiero dar,/quiero ser'[246] ('I want to see,/I want to give,/I want to be'). He provided an appealing treatment of Sondheim's line concerning the world being nothing more than an adequate 'address', adapted as 'Yesterday the world wasn't mine, I lived with no sense, I saw with no colour'.[247] In the 'Tonight Quintet', Mas-Griera translated every occurrence of the word 'tonight' as 'por fin'[248] ('finally'). Some inspired lines in his adaptation are Anita's 'He likes to make war . . . Good!/I'm going to give him war by making love' and Tony and Maria's closing phrase 'Oh, light, be light, of an endless sky with a thousand moons!'[249]

For the 'Tonight' duet, someone suggested that Serrano should retain the English word 'tonight' used twice in the first line – like Sondheim's original – and then switch to *castellano*, which would have sounded strange in a production with few English words. Instead, he combined the two ideas Mas-Griera had already chosen for 'tonight' in the duet and quintet: 'mi amor' (adding 'mi' to form '*my* love') and 'por fin'. He used the two syllables 'por fin' ('finally') 'because it is a strong word'. When Maria sings a first line of 'Mi amor, por fin' ('My love, finally') one hears a sense of certainty, and repetitions of 'por fin' in the 'Quintet' emphasises everyone's hopes.[250] (See Figure 11, for an image of the 'Quintet' in SOM's production.) Serrano, however, still finds his work with the song 'cursi' ('pretentious'). A specific lyric in his 'Tonight' that

---

[244] 'Grítalo y llenará tu alma./Cántalo y sentirás tanta calma', Serrano, p. 31.

[245] Mas-Griera, pp.17–18.   [246] Mas-Griera, p. 18.

[247] 'Ayer el mundo no era mío, vivía sin sentido, veía sin color', Mas-Griera, p. 18.

[248] Mas-Griera, pp. 30–1.

[249] 'Le gusta hacer la guerra . . . ¡Mejor!/Yo voy a darle guerra haciendo el amor', 'Oh, luz, sé luz, ¡de un cielo de mil lunas sin fin!', Mas-Griera, pp. 29–30.

[250] Serrano, pp. 34–6, 58–61.

Figure 11 The "Tonight Quintet" in SOM's production. (Photo by Javier Naval, in public domain.)

Serrano dislikes is 'nadie más que tú' ('nobody more than you'),[251] which Spaniards do not tend to say. His version of the ensemble number touches on most of the same ideas as in Sondheim's rendition with a few interesting additions. As Anita contemplates her time with Bernardo after the rumble, Serrano has her sing 'Today, nobody will bother us', and when Riff goes to Tony to make sure that he will be at the fight, he comments 'You will return to being a Jet/Finally'.[252]

In Focus's adaptation, based on the film, the Shark boys take part in 'America', with Bernardo as soloist. While in the original stage version Rosalia begins each verse, praising Puerto Rico before Anita's mocking answers, Mas-Griera follows the approach from the movie, where Anita opens each verse praising America, while Bernardo mocks her with his replies. Even though Rosalia's solo participation in the song was removed in the cinematic version, in Reguant's production, Rosalia still sang the original version's introduction. Mas-Griera retained wordplay between Rosalia's and Anita's entrances: Rosalia's vision of paradise – 'Isla de piñas y cocos,/llena de playas de ensueño,/de hombres alegres y risueños' ('Island of pineapples and coconuts,/full of dream-like beaches,/of happy and smiling men') becomes for Anita an 'Isla de pobres y locos;/llena de perros sin dueño,/llena de alegres pedigüeños' ('Island of the poor and insane,/full of dogs without owner,/full of

---

[251] Serrano, p. 34.

[252] 'Hoy nadie nos va a molestar', 'Vas a volver a ser un Jet/Por fin', Serrano, pp. 59–60.

happy beggars').[253] Interestingly, Anita later declares that 'I can live where I want' and Bernardo replies 'You will always be a foreigner!'[254] The last line of the song has Anita exclaiming to Bernardo 'You can go back swimming!' another idea paralleled by Serrano, where he makes Anita say to Rosalia 'Go back home swimming.'[255]

Serrano found 'America' 'very easy to translate' except for the constant metre changes. The opening *Tempo di seis* includes Rosalia's rapturous description of Puerto Rico followed by Anita's sarcastic riposte, if anything more bitter than the English version with lines like 'Full of tramps and rats'.[256] Once the *huapango* starts, Serrano occasionally moves lines between characters, for example allowing Anita the following opening: 'I want to be in America/I want to live in America/I feel free in America.' The fourth line of her stanza in Sondheim's original, finishing his notion about everything costing a bit in America, Serrano passes to Rosalia, who states 'Everything is a lie in America'.[257] A similar line transfer also happens in the next verse and the contrast between America and Puerto Rico in general seems starker than in the original version with Rosalia not only defending her native island but also actively attacking where she now lives, not found in Sondheim's version.

The song 'Cool' again poses a challenge in adapting to *castellano* because of its brief and broken lines formed mostly with one-syllable words. In Section 1, we noted Salvador Escamilla's striking rendition of the song into *català*, where he used the word 'noi' (literally 'boy') to replace 'boy', and 'quiet' (meaning 'still' or 'tranquil' in *català*) to replace 'get cool'. Mas-Griera and Serrano took advantage of the fact that 'boy' sounds over two notes, allowing them to add extra syllables in the text. Though neither found a one-syllable substitute for the word 'cool', Mas-Griera later in the song inserted the phrase 'Mantente frío', an effective translation of 'Just play it cool boy'.[258] Even considering the difficulties of adapting this song, Serrano found it 'simple' to translate. The feeling of his version is similar to the English, again with a bit of profanity to spice it up. One line of which Serrano is very proud in the song is: 'Respirar/Te puede salvar la vida'[259] ('To breathe/Could save your life').

'One Hand, One Heart' is another number where Mas-Griera preserved its poetic tone and general message, but not the literal meaning. He at first replaces Sondheim's idea of the couple becoming 'one' with 'I don't want to be without

---

[253] Mas-Griera, p. 15.

[254] 'Puedo vivir donde quiera', '¡Siempre serás extranjera!', Mas-Griera, p. 16.

[255] '¡Puedes volverte nadando!', Mas-Griera, p. 16; 'Puedes volverte nadando', Serrano, p. 42.

[256] 'Llena de vagos y ratas', Serrano, p. 40.

[257] 'Yo quiero estar en América/Quiero vivir en América/Me siento libre en América./Todo es mentira en América', Serrano, p. 41; Laurents/Sondheim, p. 167.

[258] Mas-Griera, p. 38; Laurents/Sondheim, p. 174.   [259] Serrano, p. 47.

you'. Even so, Mas-Griera explicitly writes in the second verse 'We are at last, you and me, one being'. Serrano reached a more faithful translation of the original song's main idea by starting with 'Make of my voice your voice'. Although 'One Hand, One Heart' is a love song, Serrano believes that he managed something 'better than the other [love songs]', but there are still lines that he dislikes. He regrets his use of 'hogar' ('home') in 'Haz de un lugar un hogar' ('Make of a place a home'),[260] a literary word that sounds out of place to him, but it rhymes with 'lugar'. When the underscoring begins, Tony and Maria recite their wedding vows, basically direct translations of the English version. The song, as few words as it is, includes several images different than those used by Sondheim, the most unusual lines being 'Make my skin your skin/ Let me be your net'.[261] Both Serrano and Mas-Griera were faithful to the original poem's irregular construction, beginning the first, second, third, and fifth lines with the same figure ('Make of our ... '/'No quiero ... ''/'Haz de mi ... '.)

Sondheim's version of 'I Feel Pretty' focuses almost exclusively on Maria singing about herself. Mas-Griera altered the original idea of Maria receiving the key to the city with her expressing the notion that 'Being pretty ... justifies that the mayor wants to make me a Miss'.[262] He has Maria's friends define her as 'Another raving lunatic in the great New York',[263] an explicit mention of the city, which never happens in the show's original text. Keeping with Serrano's typical frankness, he makes more pointed Maria's comparison of herself with other women: 'I have no rival/And I provoke/Such envy among the rest.'[264] Maria's friends are also rhetorically a bit rougher on her with their sarcasm and doubts, at one point suggesting that she has been bitten by an animal. 'I Feel Pretty' demonstrates the limits of Serrano's intentions to make as much possible use of Sondheim's rhyme schemes, assonance, and consonance. As noted in the previous section, Serrano manages a spectacular string of rhyming assonance ('Soy brillante,/Deslumbrante,/Fascinante,/Radiante'[265]), but in other places he does not, such as when he parallels Sondheim in Maria's comparison of herself with Miss America. In that sequence, Sondheim rattles off a blizzard of rhymes ('dizzy ... sunny ... fizzy ... funny'[266]), but Serrano included no rhymes in that entire stanza. In contrast, Mas-Griera showed once again an effort to preserve the way Sondheim plays with the sound of the words, weaving in, such rhymes

---

[260] Serrano, p. 57.   [261] Serrano, p. 57.

[262] 'Ser bonita ... justifica que el alcalde quiera hacerme miss', Mas-Griera, p. 26. In this case, 'miss' refers to being the winner of a beauty contest.

[263] 'Otra loca de atar en el gran Nueva York', Mas-Griera, p. 26.

[264] 'No tengo rival/y provoco/tanta envidia entre las demás', Serrano, p. 68.

[265] Serrano, p. 68.   [266] Laurents/Sondheim, p. 197.

as 'Qué perfecto/este aspecto,/inmodesto, selecto, sin par' ('How perfect/this look,/immodest, select, without equal'), and that is just one example.[267] Serrano's version of the song ends differently, with Maria singing alone rather than with her friends.

With its poetic language and profound meaning, the song 'Somewhere' was perhaps the ultimate challenge for each adaptor. Mas-Griera assigned 'Somewhere' to Tony, following the production's tendency to imitate the movie, but the video recording reveals that the final decision was for it to be sung by a female member of the ensemble, and then Tony and Maria sang the number's coda as in the original version. Mas-Griera managed to include the concepts of Tony and Maria finding their 'place' and 'time' at different places of the song, with the phrases 'There's a place beyond the sea' and 'Give us a place without time.'[268] He adapted the central ideas 'Somehow,/Someday,/ Somewhere' as 'Far,/Clean,/Free' when sung by the female voice, and as 'When?/How?/Where?'[269] when sung later by Tony and Maria, curiously articulating the questions answered in Sondheim's original. Mas-Griera also assigned these last words to Maria and Tony in their brief reprise of the song just before he dies. As explained above, after Maria's final speech, Reguant added a reprise of the whole of 'Somewhere' sung by Maria and the ensemble. The last words heard in this production were 'Far,/Clean,/Free'. Serrano retains the sense and basic meaning of Sondheim's lyrics and conveys the song's feelings of wonder and longing. The first line is the Spanish equivalent of 'Somewhere': 'En algún lugar',[270] the five syllables of that phrase demonstrating the difficulty inherent in the adaptation. Serrano's replacement of 'Somehow!/Someday!/ Somewhere!' with 'Juntos./Libres./Siempre' ('Together./Free./Always') is masterful.[271] Sondheim's rhyme scheme for the four-line stanzas in the song is aaab, which Serrano uses in the first stanza, but the others are different. Two lines still haunt Serrano: 'No habrá dolor ni mentiras/No habrá secretos ni heridas' ('There will be no pain nor lies/There will be no secrets nor injuries').[272] Serrano remembers ruefully: 'Weeks and weeks of work and we could not find another option. Very difficult, difficult!'

Mas-Griera made an excellent adaptation of 'Gee, Officer Krupke' that preserves the original meaning in notable detail, as well as its mocking tone.

---

[267] Mas-Griera, pp. 25–6.

[268] 'Más allá del mar existe un lugar', 'Dadnos un lugar sin tiempo', Mas-Griera, p. 35.

[269] Mas-Griera, p. 35.   [270] Serrano, p. 76.

[271] Laurents/Sondheim, p. 202; Serrano, pp. 76–7. This is the order of the three final words in Sondheim's version of the song as published in the piano/vocal score: Bernstein, Laurents, Sondheim, and Robbins, *West Side Story*, p. 158. In the book referenced here, the first two words are transposed.

[272] Serrano, p. 76.

As mentioned, in Focus's production the song appeared in the first act, switching locations with 'Cool', imitating the cinematic version. This placement in the movie let Riff be the main soloist (he has not died yet), but Reguant foregrounded the other Jets. As happens in Mas-Griera's adaptation of spoken dialogues, ironic expressions became more explicit insults. He translated 'Gee, Officer Krupke' as 'Hey, don't fuck with me, Krupke'.[273] (Serrano created the hook for his version inspired by the ironic treatment of the original version's first line: 'Dear kindly Sergeant Krupke', which became 'Querido Sargento', or 'Dear Sergeant'.)[274] For the song's last line, Mas-Griera adapted 'Krup you!' as '¡Cabrón!' ('Bastard!'), recovering Sondheim's original intention of closing this number with a strong epithet.[275] Mas-Griera's adaptation follows to the letter excuses provided by the juvenile delinquent to justify his behaviour, including specific mentions of his dysfunctional family. Sondheim's verse about family members became as 'My mother is a slut,/My father is a snitch,/My grandma is a drug addict,/My grandpa is a dumbass,/My sister is a dyke,/My brother is a faggot./Sons of bitches, what a mess!'[276] Again the anaphora is preserved, together with the meaning, although with a more direct and aggressive tone than the original. Throughout the song, Sondheim delivered an interesting message by inserting conclusions made by the Jets at the end of each verse, starting with 'there is good' (what they try to tell society) and concluding with 'we're no good' (how society judges them). This idea is somewhat lost in both adaptations, where Mas-Griera started with 'there is goodness' and ends with 'to prison', and Serrano wrote 'I have love' and 'I'm Satan' respectively.[277] Serrano reports that he enjoyed working on 'Gee, Officer Krupke', an opportunity to play with the language in numerous verses. He preserves the song's essential jocularity, tells the story, and incorporates the social commentary. It is another number where it was not possible to follow Sondheim's rhyme scheme throughout.

'A Boy Like That' is violent in any language with music that rivals 'The Rumble' in intensity and metric variety. Mas-Griera adapted the initial line with 'Un chico así',[278] literal translation of the song's title, though less effective than

---

[273] 'Eh, no joda, Krupke', Mas-Griera, pp. 20–2.   [274] Serrano, pp. 79–83.

[275] Sondheim's original line for this moment, 'Fuck you', is the one that provoked a negative reaction among producers, as mentioned above.

[276] 'Mi madre es una furcia,/Mi padre es un soplón,/Mi abuela es drogadicta,/Mi abuelo es un mamón./Mi hermana es tortillera,/Mi hermano, maricón./Hijoputas, ¡vaya confusión!' This is the verse as heard in the recording of the performance; a different text appears in Mas-Griera's version.

[277] 'Hay bondad', 'A prisión', Mas-Griera, pp. 20–1; 'Tengo amor', 'Soy Satán', Serrano, pp. 80, 82.

[278] Mas-Griera, p. 39.

Serrano's opening, 'El muy cabrón', commented on above. Sondheim wrote a text with strong imagery, but again Serrano went even further. After his opening line, Serrano includes such images as 'A man like that will tear the heart' and 'A man like that is a sick one/You will live in hell'.[279] Sondheim rhymes the first two lines in each A section, a construction that Serrano imitates. In the B section, the writers use different rhyme schemes.

As a connection between 'A boy like that' and the second part of this number, 'I have a love', Sondheim had Maria remind Anita that she also loved a boy prone to violence. Mas-Griera wrote here 'It happened to you, too./You already know', but Serrano abandoned this idea, simply writing 'Listen to me, he's not like that./You don't know him'.[280]

In Maria's eloquent answer to Anita, 'I Have a Love', Mas-Griera adapted the title phrase as 'Es solo amor' ('It's only love'), and by Serrano as 'Tengo su amor' ('I have his love').[281] The fact that neither resorted to the easiest and more literal translation, 'Tengo un amor', suggests that both authors sought to preserve the poetic tone. It is also possible that each avoided the obvious translation because it sounds rather clumsy with the music. This song includes more dramatic imagery in Serrano's version, with Maria stating that each of them would die for the other. Sondheim's version is a bit more dependent upon rhyme than Serrano's translation, but both are strong declarations. In the three lines of duet for Maria and Anita that close the song, Sondheim describes the strength of the couple's love, rendering moot choices of right and wrong. These lines provide a last, fine example of the different approaches followed by the two adaptors. Mas-Griera found a translation that preserves the original meaning and rhyme scheme of aab (using the same word, 'amor', to rhyme the first and second lines): 'Si es fuerte el amor,/No hay buen o mal amor,/¡Amar es vivir!'[282] ('If love is strong, there's no good or bad love. To love is to live!'). For his adaptation, Serrano chose instead a phrase that sounds more natural, though with a slightly different meaning about love that 'escapes your control', allowing one to know that it is real: 'Y cuando el amor/escapa a tu control/tu amor es real'[283] ('And when love escapes your control, your love is real'). Serrano's rhyme scheme is abc versus Sondheim's aab, a final symbol of the broader choices afforded the initial creator of the lyrics versus the adaptor's need to balance a song's meaning and emotional quality while also searching for words and images in another language that will speak to an audience aesthetically.

---

[279] 'Un hombre así te va a arrancar el corazón', 'Un hombre así es un enfermo/Vas a vivir en un infierno', Serrano, p. 87.

[280] 'A ti también te sucedió./Tú ya lo sabes', Mas-Griera, p. 40; 'Escúchame, él no es así./No lo conoces', Serrano, p. 88.

[281] Mas-Griera, p. 40; Serrano, p. 88.   [282] Mas-Griera, p. 40.   [283] Serrano, p. 89.

Our analysis of two adaptations of the iconic text by Laurents and Sondheim showcases the many complexities that occur when adapting a musical for audiences distant from the show's original time and space. The possibility of using the original English text is not viable for such a production in Spain, so the language – and hence the work – has to be transformed, a rule that applies almost systematically to every Anglo-American production that crosses international and/or language borders. In this case, the mere notion of a translation into *castellano* already defies the original concept of using the language of the story's protagonists – young members of New York street gangs that speak English with a particular type of slang. To add another level of difficulty, some characters make sporadic use of Spanish, which not only portrays ethnicity but also helps to underline the clash between cultures. As noted above, the 2009 Broadway revival of *West Side Story* offered a closer attempt at this reality with more lines spoken and sung in Spanish by Puerto Rican characters, adapted by Lin-Manuel Miranda. Audiences disliked the idea and many lines reverted back to English, suggesting that audiences do not necessarily value authenticity over familiarity and understanding the entire text.[284]

When adapting the work for modern Spanish audiences, Mas-Griera and Serrano searched for solutions that preserved the story's dramatic content. Both used language that sounded natural for the characters portrayed: violent youth gangs with members unable to fit into society, with two lovers among them. One consequence was extensive use of profanity in both adaptations, which adds a new touch of authenticity to the original text. Neither of these Spanish productions included a distinction between the languages spoken by rival gangs.

Even with these similarities, these two adaptations illustrate different approaches. While Focus's production imitated the 1961 cinematic version, the main telling of the work known by Spanish audiences, SOM hewed as closely as possible to the original theatrical production. Mas-Griera modified the text to follow changes made for the film, while Serrano remained faithful to the original, making slight cuts that he judged necessary to avoid an unnatural use of the language.

Regarding the song's lyrics, both adaptors made strong efforts to fit Spanish words into Bernstein's melodies while imitating aspects of Sondheim's poetry. While they achieved correct placement of accents and a sense of naturalness in both adaptations, we have demonstrated contrasting results in the preservation of rhyme schemes and meaning, mainly in songs with high poetic content or those dominated by short melodic phrases. The many differences we have

---

[284] Gans, 'A Song Like That'.

extracted from this comparison of adaptations provide a revealing example of the broad variety of choices available to an adaptor, even when translating a source to the same language for audiences of the same country.

7 Steven Spielberg's *West Side Story* Arrives in Spain (2021)

Steven Spielberg fell in love with the music of *West Side Story* at the age of ten when his parents purchased the original cast album of the 1957 Broadway production, and he had long dreamed of directing his own version of the story on film.[285] Except for single scenes in *Indiana Jones and the Temple of Doom* and *1941*, Spielberg had little experience directing musical sequences. His collaborators for *West Side Story* included choreographer Justin Peck, supervising vocal producer Jeanine Tesori, conductor Gustavo Dudamel (leading the New York and Los Angeles Philharmonics), and screenwriter Tony Kushner.

West Side Story is justifiably famous in the history of the American musical, but it has often been criticised for cultural insensitivities found in the work and its production, including, for example: the negative characterisation of Puerto Ricans in general and the island of Puerto Rico specifically in the song 'America'; the frequent use of white actors to portray Puerto Ricans – the case with the majority of characters in both the original Broadway version and film; and the use of brownface makeup on the actors in the original film; among other issues. Spielberg set out to correct some of these problems. He consulted with members of the Puerto Rican community about many aspects of life and representation and allowed his cast, which included twenty Puerto Rican actors – eight hired in San Juan – to remain with their own skin tones, showing the diversity of pigmentation known on the island.[286] The film included the 'America' lyrics from the 1961 film (with one offensive line changed by Sondheim) instead of the Broadway original, somewhat softening the criticism of Puerto Rico as a place to live. Kushner's screenplay included numerous small changes to the story, such as making Maria a bit older and less naïve and allowing the Puerto Rican characters to speak a great deal of Spanish, which Spielberg presented without subtitles. This latter step constitutes a major political statement in the United States, making Spanish equally important to English in the film. This was one of the aspects in the film that caused some conservative elements to consider it to be *woke*, a term originating in the African American community that designates one sensitive to societal injustice, especially racism. For the right wing it has become a label of derision directed at liberals.

---

[285] 'Steven Spielberg Dishes'.   [286] Lee, 'Commentary'.

The show's score received a faithful reading, with almost every section from Bernstein's music sounding somewhere in the film but with some songs placed in different dramatic situations. The cast includes Rachel Zegler as Maria, Ansel Elgort as Tony, Ariana DeBose as Anita, David Alvarez as Bernardo, Mike Faist as Riff, and Rita Moreno (Anita in the original film) as Valentina, a replacement character for Doc. Iris Menas, a trans actor, played Anybodys as a trans character.

West Side Story's release in the United States occurred on 10 December 2021. Critics mostly reacted positively, some ecstatically. Brian Tallerico, for example, loved the film except for the casting of Ansel Elgort: 'Kushner and Spielberg have stayed loyal to the play and original film while also making notable changes in a way that makes it fresh and vibrant. And they have staged their production in a way that's often mesmerizing. One misguided casting decision holds it back from absolute greatness.'[287] Despite many rave reviews, however, the film proved disappointing in drawing viewers as the Omicron variant of COVID-19 surged; total box office totalled only $36.6 million in its first three weeks.[288]

Spielberg's *West Side Story* premiered in Spanish cinemas on 22 December 2021, with a grand preview in Madrid on 14 December in the cinema Palacio de la Prensa, which many celebrities attended. The film has been screened in its original version (with subtitles for the English dialogues and lyrics) and in a dubbed version. A trailer posted on YouTube by 20th Century Studios España on 15 September 2021[289] reveals a first intention of using a standard dubbing with all the characters speaking *español neutro*.[290] The film was finally presented with a mixed dubbing, which was revealed when the production studio posted another trailer on 3 December.[291] All of the dialogue by Puerto Rican characters has been dubbed by Puerto Rican actors; this dubbing is shared with the Latin American versions of the film.[292] The remainder of the spoken lines was dubbed in *español neutro*. Sung parts have not been dubbed.

The decision to use a mixed dubbing has a decisive impact on one's perception of the film. Even when all characters speak Spanish, there is still a sharp contrast between the Puerto Ricans and the rest of the characters. To the ears of a Spanish spectator, the Puerto Ricans display a strong accent and a distinctive

---

[287] Tallerico, '*West Side Story*'.   [288] Whitten, 'With just $36.6 million'.

[289] '*West Side Story*', www.youtube.com/watch?v=sx3_DqF-14s.

[290] A variant of Spanish that is used commonly in dubbed products, designed to suppress any identification with specific Spanish-speaking regions by avoiding distinctive accents and idioms.

[291] '*West Side Story*', www.youtube.com/watch?v=Q2Pg67Hfz3Q.

[292] See 'Amor sin barreras (2021)'.

use of language, with abundant idioms and grammar rules that are not shared in Spain. In a country where cinema is systematically marketed in dubbed versions, this mixed dubbing stands out as an innovative attempt to respect the original idea of authenticity and inclusiveness of the film.[293]

All in all, the entire adaptation of the spoken text to Spanish, with practically no use of English words, has failed to solve some situations. There are several moments where Anita and other characters ask someone else to speak in English, a request that has been lost in the dubbed version. For example, in the scene when Lt Schrank is interviewing Maria and Anita, and the girls try to speak in Spanish so he cannot understand them, Schrank simply demands 'Más alto' ('Speak louder') instead of the original 'In English'. The result is even more awkward in a scene where Tony writes down in Spanish some romantic phrases for Maria that Valentina teaches him, a dialogue that simply makes no sense in the dubbed version. The only explicit reference to an idiomatic difference between cultures is shown in a dialogue between Bernardo and Anita, when he says that Tony is 'un Polack' (instead of 'un polaco') and Anita replies '¡Polack, dice el spic! ¡Ahora sí suenas como un americano!' ('Polack, says the spic! Now you sound like an American!'), literally translating her remark.

Among the nineteen Spanish press reviews consulted, twelve were positive (with five raves), five mixed, and two negatives. Most of the reviews include multiple comparisons with Wise's film. Reviewers focused mostly on the question concerning Spielberg's success or failure in his attempt to respect and pay homage to the original material but, at the same time, offer something new. Luis Martínez, in his praise for the film in *Metropoli*, claims that Spielberg has succeeded in bringing back Wise's film 'intact' but giving the spectator a feeling of watching *West Side Story* again for the first time.[294] Mireia Mullor from *Fotogramas* offers that the best feature of the remake is 'its ability to be at the same time classic and modern, nostalgic and refreshing'.[295] While a reviewer from *Noticias de Gipuzkoa* sees the film as an anachronism and an unnecessary remake,[296] Carlos Marañón declares in *Cinemania* that 'Spielberg achieves something that seemed impossible: blowing a deserved raspberry to the sceptics, his adaptation seems justified in the end'.[297] Sergi Sánchez's words for *La Razón* sum up the best and worst features of the film commented upon in

---

[293] It is worth mentioning two recent films that could have contributed to this initiative: *Coco* (2017) and *Encanto* (2021). Both were distributed in Spain preserving their Latin American dubbing, a logical decision since all the characters from *Coco* are Mexican and those from *Encanto* are Colombian. These two films and Spielberg's *West Side Story* were distributed by the Walt Disney Company, which could have been responsible for such decisions.

[294] Martínez, '*West Side Story*'.   [295] Mullor, 'Crítica de "*West Side Story*"'.

[296] 'Críticas de cine / "*West Side Story*."'   [297] Marañón, 'Crítica de "*West Side Story*"'.

the majority of reviews: 'The best: The political dimension of Spielberg's proposal and the delicious neoclassical aroma of the mise-en-scène. The worst: That it has the appearance of an unnecessary remake.'[298] Several reviewers highlighted the technical aspects of the film, most notably Ignacio Aguilar in his thorough analysis of the photographic techniques.[299]

Though Javier González de la Huebra lamented that 'it would have been more interesting as a new version updated to the current times, offering a different vision than that of the fifties',[300] some of the reviewers remarked that the social and political issues portrayed in the story are still relevant. It is especially interesting to note Mariona Gumpert's review for *Vozpópuli*, which includes an extensive comment on the *woke* phenomenon and the historical relevance of events shown in the film.[301] In *Espinof*, Víctor López claims that the film has updated the original work's 'content, nuances, themes and form to these days', but later adds: 'Despite its face-lift, I strongly doubt that *West Side Story* will attract the youngest audience to the cinema theatres – in fact, the musical is not a genre that is a good friend with the box office.'[302]

Interestingly, only a few reviewers commented on the dubbing, projecting general disapproval: 'It is a crime to screen in one language a film in which the clash between cultures is a central part of the plot.'[303] Still, none of them mention the mixed dubbing. A quick exploration through online forums reveals contrasting reactions that range from approval to confusion.[304] One must remember that this type of dubbing is still new for the Spanish audience, who perhaps needs time to become accustomed to it.

Since this is a film that is still less than two months old as these lines are written, it is too soon to evaluate its long-term impact on the Spanish – and international – culture. At the very least, it is a proof that the artistic and sociocultural debates opened by *West Side Story* since its theatrical premiere remain alive and fresh more than sixty years later.

Conclusion

It is widely acknowledged that *West Side Story* was a revolutionary piece of American musical theatre that has left a permanent mark on American culture. After studying the show's life in Spain, we can safely say that the artistic and cultural impact of this work also resonated elsewhere, while being subject to different kinds of adaptation. Spanish culture embraced *West*

---

[298] Sánchez, 'Crítica de "*West Side Story*"'.   [299] Aguilar, '*West Side Story*'.
[300] González de la Huebra Sánchez, 'Crítica de "*West Side Story*"'.
[301] Gumpert, '*West Side Story*'.   [302] López G. '*West Side Story*'.   [303] Gumpert.
[304] See, for example: www.foroseldoblaje.com/foro/viewtopic.php?t=83210 and
      www.forocoches.com/foro/showthread.php?t=8876794.

Side Story first through its film, a striking presence in terms of permanence in cinemas and high praise from critics. With no access to a theatrical production for decades, the film became the work's main reference for the Spanish audience. Nevertheless, Spanish audiences and artists acknowledged the property's quality beyond cinemas. Bernstein's music for *West Side Story* found a permanent place in live concerts and recordings, and this composer has been revered in Spanish culture, mainly for this work. When touring productions reached Spain in the 1980s, the show was already considered an iconic work of high quality. Accordingly, some of these performances were the highlight of major events, like summer festivals. Although audiences and critics mostly received these productions warmly, they do not seem to have had a lasting effect on the knowledge of the work by Spaniards, for whom the film remained as the ultimate reference. This was a decisive fact when Focus put together the first local production of *West Side Story* in the 1990s. However, it was no longer an issue two decades later, when SOM offered the first adaptation into Spanish that was faithful to the original Broadway production – even while reissuing the film on DVD as a promotional strategy.

We have gathered valuable information on how the adaptation of an American musical has worked in another country. Spaniards had direct contact with the original English text through the film and its soundtrack recording. During the first year and a half of its screening in Spain, the film was not dubbed; later dubbing sounded for spoken dialogue. This is significant in a country where dubbing has always been the norm for foreign films. On the other hand, when local artists recorded the show's most popular songs in the 1960s, translators adapted the texts to *castellano* and *català*, proving the value of understanding lyrics even when the songs sound on a recording, isolated from the story. The arrival of the new film version in 2021, bilingual in nature, provided an innovative solution in the process of dubbing by using two con-trasting variants of Spanish, a practice that still sounds strange to the Spanish audience.

The two major adaptations of *West Side Story* by local creative teams demonstrate that there are many variables to consider when redesigning it for the Spanish market. In a period when the Anglo-American musical as a genre was still taking off in Spain, Reguant imitated the film as closely as possible, taking advantage of the audience's familiarity with the material. For practical reasons, Reguant also had to abandon the initial idea of adapting the show to *català*. Albert Mas-Griera worked out a careful, intelligent adaptation, cleaving closely to the original text – excepting the modifications copied from the cinematic version. SOM Produce prepared its version of the show in an especially favourable moment for the genre in Spain, the rendition premiering in Madrid next to several other major productions of American and Spanish musicals. SOM conceived this adaptation as an opportunity to offer Spanish audiences for the first time the original theatrical experience of *West Side Story*. David Serrano added a new touch to his adaptation of the text by making it sound more natural in *castellano*, and the team offered an interpretation of the characters that made them realistic and appealing. In these two productions we find two contrasting ways of updating a show by adapting it to a different time and place while trying to preserve its original flavour.

West Side Story became a masterpiece of musical cinema in Spain and soon achieved the status of a timeless work of art, be it on the screen, in the concert hall, or on stage. In all forms and settings, it has delivered a universal message that speaks to audiences of different times, in a country where juvenile delinquency, immigration issues and impossible love stories also exist – and Shakespeare's work is of course well known.

Bibliography

Aguilar, I. '*West Side Story*', www.harmonicacinema.com/west-side-story-2021///, accessed 28 January 2022.

Alonso, G. 'Discos/Comedia musical: Bernstein, al frente de su *West Side Story*', *El País*, 1 June 1985, supl. Artes, p. 7.

Alvarado, E. '*West Side* madrileño', *El Mundo del Siglo Veintiuno*, 24 June 2009, supl. M2, p. 8.

'Amor sin barreras (2021)', https://doblaje.fandom.com/es/wiki/Amor_sin_barreras_(2021), accessed 28 January 2022.

'ANOTACIONES con ALBERT MAS-GRIERA', interview with *Anotaciones*, 29 November 2020, www.youtube.com/watch?v=Y5nS2chAHG8, accessed 3 July 2021.

A. Q. '*West Side Story* (Capitol)', *El Eco de Canarias*, 26 July 1964, p. 4.

'Aribau Cinema. 8 semanas clamorosas. *West Side Story*' [advertisement], *El Mundo Deportivo*, 4 February 1963, p. 11.

Avello, 'Real Cinema: *West Side Story (Amor sin barreras)*', *La Nueva España*, 31 December 1963, pp. 5, 8.

Ayanz, M. 'Todo es posible en América', *La Razón*, 4 July 2009.

Bejarano, F. '*West Side Story*, canto a la nostalgia', *Diario 16*, 9 October 1983, p. 40.

Beltran, A. 'Una compañía de Broadway representa en Valencia *West Side Story*', *El País*, 29 February 1988, p. 31.

Benach, J.-A. '¡Danzad, danzad, pandillas!' *La Vanguardia*, 19 December 1996, p. 54.

Bernstein, L., A. Laurents, S. Sondheim, and J. Robbins, *West Side Story* (New York: G. Schirmer and Chappell & Co., Inc., 1957, 1959).

Bernstein, L., S. Sondheim, 'América', Piano/vocal score, trans. C. Mapel (pseudonym for Augusto Algueró), Canciones del Mundo, 1964.

Bernstein, L., S. Sondheim, 'María', Piano/vocal score, trans. C. Mapel (pseudonym for Augusto Algueró), Canciones del Mundo, 1962.

Bernstein, L., S. Sondheim, '¡Qué noche!' ('Tonight'), Piano/vocal score, trans. C. Mapel (pseudonym for Augusto Algueró), Canciones del Mundo, 1962.

Blanco, R. 'Bodas de oro de *West Side Story*', *Mundo Clásico*, 4 September 2009.

Blanco, R. '"Tony y Maria", iconos en Santander', *El Diario Montañés*, 23 August 2009, p. 73.

Bravo, J. 'Broadway se instala en la Casa de Campo', *ABC*, 24 June 2009, p. 63.

Bravo, J. 'El genuino sabor americano', *ABC*, 29 June 2009.

Bravo, J. 'Fieles al espíritu coreográfico original de Jerome Robbins', *ABC*, 20 December 1997, p. 97.

Bravo, J. 'Focus sube al Nuevo Apolo el gran musical *West Side Story*', *ABC*, 13 December 1997, p. 93.

Bravo, J. 'Respetuoso con el original', *Diario ABC.com*, 5 October 2018.

'Broadway llega a Asturias', *La Nueva España*, supl. *El Paraíso*, 25 August 2009, p. 1.

Bueno, G. '*West Side Story*, comedia musical norteamericana, triunfa en Londres', *Falange*, 20 December 1958, p. 5.

Burgueño, J. P. 'Gimnasia dorada', *El Correo Español*, 3 August 1996, supl. *Atlanta*, p. 9.

C. 'Versión española de *West Side Story*', *El Mundo Deportivo*, 24 June 1964, p. 5.

Calvache, V. '*West Side Story*, música y lágrimas en la Plaza Vieja', *La Voz de Almería*, 12 August 1988, p. 15.

Cararach, J. A. 'Apuesta bien resuelta', *El Periódico de Catalunya*, 18 December 1996, p. 57.

'Carta del Director', *Programa de Mano*, SOM Produce production of *West Side Story*, 2018, p. [5].

Castillejo, R. 'El amor no tiene tiempo', *Sevilla Magazine*, 9 January 2019.

Centeno, E. 'Aquel Barrio Oeste de Nueva York', *Diario 16*, 21 December 1997, p. 51.

'Cine Paz celebra su 75 aniversario con un ciclo de grandes obras maestras', *La Vanguardia*, 2 November 2018, www.lavanguardia.com/vida/20181102/452685656709/cine-paz-celebra-su-75-aniversario-con-un-ciclo-de-grandes-obras-maestras.html, accessed 12 July 2021.

'Cinema Paz: *West Side Story*' [advertisement], *ABC*, 1 March 1963, p. 28.

'Crece el número de espectadores de teatro en el primer trimestre', *La Vanguardia*, 19 April 1997, p. 50.

'Críticas de cine / *West Side Story*: Chicos de barrio', 31 December 2021, www.noticiasdegipuzkoa.eus/cultura/2021/12/31/chicos-barrio/1171340.html/, accessed 28 January 2022.

Crowther, B. 'Gypsies and Flamenco in *Los Tarantos*', *New York Times*, 30 June 1964.

C. T. 'Más de treinta bailarines protagonizan el musical *West Side Story* en San Sebastián', *El Correo Español*, 31 July 1997, p. 36.

'Desde hace casi cinco meses, un éxito sensacional', *El Mundo Deportivo*, 14 April 1963, p. 10.

Díez-Crespo, M. 'Crítica de teatro: *Maruxa*, en la Zarzuela', *Primer Plano*, 29 March 1963, p. 42.

Duran, L. 'La América de *West Side Story* llega a Palma', *Diario de Mallorca*, 19 March 1998, p. 53.

'El domingo llegará a Barcelona el actor George Chakiris', *El Mundo Deportivo*, 28 February 1964, p. 8.

Eslake, S. 'Donald Chan has conducted more than 3,000 performances of *West Side Story* and he's back for more', CutCommon: The New Generation of Classical Music, 28 March 2019, www.cutcommonmag.com/donald-chan-has-conducted-more-than-3000-performances-of-west-side-story2/, accessed 4 October 2020.

Fernández, E. 'Tema y pensamiento: Preferimos la "anticuada" Europa', *Proa*, 5 April 1964, p. 7.

Fernández-Cid, A. 'Discos: Dos publicaciones de particular interés', *Blanco y Negro*, 20 April 1963, p. 116.

Figaredo, D. 'Amores que matan', *La Voz de Asturias*, 26 August 2009, p. 64.

Formentor, M. B. 'Peligros emboscados', *La Vanguardia*, 19 December 1996, p. 54.

'France', *Cash Box*, 22, no. 51, 2 September 1961, p. 41.

Fresno, N. 'Crítica: *West Side Story*, cuando lo "vintage" es historia del género musical (y de la danza y la música)', *Shangay.com*, 21 October 2018.

Furia, P. and M. Lasser, *America's Songs: The Stories Behind the Songs of Broadway, Hollywood, and Tin Pan Alley* (New York: Routledge, 2008).

Gans, A. 'A song like that: collaborators reconsider Spanish lyrics in *West Side Story*', *Playbill*, 25 August 2009, www.playbill.com/article/a-song-like-that-collaborators-reconsider-spanish-lyrics-in-west-side-story-com-163835, accessed 14 June 2021.

Garcia Garzon, J. I. 'Crítica de teatro: *West Side Story*, veintiséis años después', *ABC*, 7 October 1983, p. 77.

García Jiménez, L. '*West Side Story*, un film que causará profundo impacto', *Diario de Las Palmas*, 25 January 1964, p. 4.

García-Requena, F. 'Romeo y Julieta (versión 1961)', *Blanco y Negro*, 22 April 1961, p. 40–4.

García-Requena, F. '*West Side Story*, una obra maestra del cine norteamericano', *Blanco y Negro*, 21 April 1962, p. 44–8.

Gea, J. C. 'Estación Broadway: Tren diurno desde el *West Side*', *La Nueva España*, 17 July 1997, supl. *El Paraíso*, pp. 1, 4–5.

Gea, J. C. 'Gijón cantó "América"', *La Nueva España*, 18 July 1997, supl. *El Paraíso*, p. 3.

Ginart, B. 'Pobres emigrantes', *El País*, 29 November 1996, supl. *El País de las Tentaciones*, p. 19.

González, J.-J. '*West Side Story* se despide de Madrid para salir de gira', *Broadway World Spain*, 3 April 2019, www.broadwayworld.com/spain/art icle/WEST-SIDE-STORY-se-despide-de-Madrid-para-salir-de-gira-20190403, accessed 1 November 2020.

González de la Huebra Sánchez, J. 'Crítica de *West Side Story* (2021): I Like to Be in America … Again!', 22 December 2021, https://cinefilosfrustrados .com/west-side-story-critica-2021///, accessed 28 January 2022.

González Echevarría, M. N., '*West Side Story* y su doble filo', *Primer Plano*, 8 March 1963, p. 3.

Gumpert, M. '*West Side Story*: la importancia de los lazos y afectos', 26 December 2021, www.vozpopuli.com/altavoz/cultura/west-side-story .html//, accessed 28 January 2022.

Haro Tecglen, E. 'Odiosa comparación', *El País*, 23 December 1997, p. 38.

Hontañón, R. 'Vigor, vigencia y dinamismo, una Vuelta de tuerca a *West Side Story*', *El Diario Montañés*, 24 August 2009, p. 68.

Intxausti, A. 'El musical *West Side Story* abre la programación de los Veranos de la Villa', *El País*, 26 June 2009, p. 82.

'La ópera *West Side Story* triunfó ante la juventud cántabra', *Diario 16*, 20 August 1988, supl. *Verano y Humo*, p. 4.

Lee, A. 'Commentary: Spielberg tried to save *West Side Story*. But its history makes it unsalvageable', *Los Angeles Times*, 12 December 2021, www .latimes.com/entertainment-arts/movies/story/2021-12-12/west-side-story-puerto-rico-cultural-authenticity, accessed 21 January 2022.

'Leonard Bernstein mantiene a su musa en activa', *La Provincia*, 25 August 1988, p. 40.

López G., V. '*West Side Story*: Steven Spielberg y Janusz Kaminski hacen confluir presente y pasado en un musical excepcional', 27 December 2021, www.espinof.com/estrenos/west-side-story-steven-spielberg-janusz-kaminski-hacen-confluir-presente-pasado-musical-excepcional, accessed 28 January 2022.

López Sancho, L. '*West Side Story*, un musical de siempre', *ABC*, 20 December 1997, p. 97.

'Los Premios San Jorge de Cinematografía 1962', *¡Hola!*, 12 October 1963, p. 36.

Manuel Burell, V. 'MUSICA MODERNA: Estreno de *West Side Story*'. *Cinco Días*, 8 October 1983, p. 23.

Marañón, C. 'Crítica de *West Side Story*', 20 December 2021, www.20minu tos.es/cinemania/criticas/critica-de-west-side-story-4929520//, accessed 28 January 2022.

Marco, T. 'LEONARD BERNSTEIN, la madurez de un mito', *Diario 16*, 25 August 1983, p. 15.

Marías, J. '*West Side Story*', *Gaceta Ilustrada*, 15 September 1962, p. 23.

Marin-Hidalgo, M. 'La opinión del crítico: Rambla: *West Side Story*', *Sabadell*, 16 February 1965, p. 7.

Marinero, C. 'Romeo y Julieta del Bronx', *El Mundo del Siglo Veintiuno*, 19 June 2009, supl. *La Luna de Metrópoli*, p. 41.

Martínez, C. J. 'Un clásico inolvidable', *La Nueva España*, supl. *El Paraíso*, 27 August 2009, pp. 1–2.

Martínez, L. '*West Side Story*: Y bailaré sobre la tumba del tiempo', 2 December 2021, www.elmundo.es/metropoli/cine/2021/12/02/61a8a82fe4d4d89c298b45 ba.html, accessed 28 January 2022.

Martínez Tomas, A. 'Inauguración de *Aribau Cinema*: Estreno del film *West Side Story* (Amor sin barreras)', *La Vanguardia Española*, 9 December 1962, p. 45.

Mas-Griera, A. Email interview with the authors, September 2021.

Mas-Griera, A. [adaptor], *West Side Story*. Libreto Arthur Laurents. Música Leonard Bernstein. Letras Stephen Sondheim. Adaptación Albert Mas-Griera.

Matas, R. 'Madison Spain's Summer Delight' and 'Duo Dinamico Takes Song Prize', *Billboard Music Week*, 1 September 1962, pp. 17–18.

Mateo, M. 'Anglo-American Musicals in Spanish Theatres', *Translation and Music*, ed. Sebnem Susam-Saraeva, *The Translator*, 14, 2 (2008), pp. 319–42.

Mier, L. 'Aún y siempre la historia del *West Side*', *Alerta*, 25 August 2009, p. 56.

Mori, A. '#PlanesLook/*West Side Story* llega a Madrid: Derrítete con la historia de amor de Tony y María', *OKDiario.com*, 10 October 2018.

Moya, E., J. L. Guarner, J. Parejo Díaz, J. Cobos, J. L. García Sánchez, J. Munsó Cabús, 'Nada más que la verdad de *West Side Story*', *Film Ideal*, 116, 15 March 1963, pp. 186–90.

Mullor, M. 'Crítica de *West Side Story*', 20 December 2021, www.fotogramas .es/peliculas-criticas/a38566534/west-side-story-critica-pelicula/, accessed 28 January 2022.

Muñoz-Rojas, R. '*West Side Story* acerca un trozo del Bronx neoyorquino en español', *El País*, 18 December 1997, supl. *Madrid*, p. 7.

Nieto, L. '*West Side Story*, el gran musical de Broadway en Madrid', *FamiliasActivas.com*, 6 January 2019.

'Opinión de *West Side Story* El Musical', *PaseandoaMissCultura.com*, 8 October 2018.

Orive, J. 'Un musical de tono acertado y correcto', *La Provincia*, 9 October 1997, p. 18.

Orive, J. '*West Side Story*: Romeo y Julieta en Nueva York' *La Provincia*, 7 October 1997, p. 20.

Otheguy Riveira, H. '*West Side Story*: un gran musical en perfecta tormenta de violencia y romanticismo', *Culturamas.es*, 7 October 2018.

Palomar, J. R. 'Víctor Ullate Roda', *Tiempo* 24 February 1997, pp. 110–11.

Pascual, I. 'Baile de bandas en Chamartín', *El Mundo del Siglo Veintiuno*, 13 December 1997, supl. *Madrid*, p. 1.

Patterson, M. *75 Años de historia del musical en España (1930–2005)* (Madrid: Ediciones y Publicaciones, 2010).

Paul, '*West Side Story* en el Cinema Paz', *Marca*, 2 March 1963, p. 10.

Peñafiel, P. 'George Chakiris se considera un hombre reservado, pero no tímido', *La Nueva España*, 8 March 8, p. 19.

Pérez de Olaguer, G. 'Cita de amor y muerte en el Tívoli', *El Periódico de Catalunya*, 2 December 1996, p. 33.

Pérez de Olaguer, G. 'Llega un potente *West Side Story*', *El Periódico de Catalunya*, 28 November 1996, p. 61.

Pérez de Olaguer, G. 'Reencuentro con un mítico musical', *El Periódico de Catalunya*, 17 December 1996, p. 61.

Pérez de Pablos, S. 'Me gusta vivir en América . . . ', *El País*, 28 April 1996, p. 68.

'Primer aniversario de Aribau Cinema' [advertisement], *El Mundo Deportivo*, 9 December 1963, p. 11.

'Primeros espadas sobre el scenario en el patio de butacas', *La Nueva España*, 28 August 2009, p. 62.

'Publicidad USA en español: "Todo es mejor en América" ', *Expansión*, 15 August 1988, p. 19.

Puiche, G. 'El último estreno de la temporada en Broadway: *West Side Story*, versión neoyorquina de *Romeo y Julieta*', *La Hora*, 28 November 1957, pp. 15–16.

Rami, A. 'Mejor imposible', *Teatro Madrid.com*, 21 October 2018.

Reguant, R. '1996 *West Side Story*' [online], Ricard Reguant blog, http://ricardre guant.blogspot.com/2010/04/1996-west-side-story.html, accessed 14 June 2021.

Reguant, R. *WEST SIDE STORY* (1er acto), www.youtube.com/watch? v=nDZJZWTwi-w, accessed 14 June 2021.

Reguant, R. *WEST SIDE STORY* (2º acto). www.youtube.com/watch?v=VGe-R6M0ri8, accessed 14 June 2021.

Roba, S. and G. Arroyo, 'Madrid se llenó de estrellas', *Diario 16*, 1 November 1996, supl. *Campeones 16*, p. 8.

Roger, B. '*West Side Story*: Treinta años de su estreno', *Diario de Las Palmas*, 4 September 1988, supl. *Mujer*, pp. 1, 24.

R. T. '*West Side Story* de Robert Wise y Jerome Robbins', *Sabadell*, 19 March 1963, p. 4.

Ruiz, A. '*West Side Story* en el Teatro Calderón: Apuesta rotunda por el clasicismo en esta magnífica adaptación de uno de los grandes musicales de la historia', *El Teatrero*, 4 October 2018.

Rullán, M. 'Las españolas consiguieron, en una tarde de gloria, el oro más hermoso', *La Provincia*, 3 August 1996, p. 36.

Sabater, M. 'A la ratlla de la involució', *Diari de Sabadell*, 2 December 1997, p. 48.

Sagré, J. '*West Side Story*, gigantesco espectáculo de mucha enjundia humana', *El Mundo Deportivo*, December 7, 1962, p. 8.

Sagré, J. '*West Side Story*: La película que sólo podía producir el cine americano', *El Mundo Deportivo*, 10 January 1964, p. 8.

Salgueiro, J. B. 'Las bandas rivales de *West Side Story* se enfrentan en Santiago', *Faro de Vigo*, 25 July 1997, supl. *Verano del 97*, p. 4.

San Agustín, A. 'Alba Quezada, cantante y actriz', *El Periódico de Catalunya*, 15 December 1996, p. 9.

Sánchez, S. 'Crítica de *West Side Story*: amor en ruinas', 21 December 2021, www.larazon.es/cultura/20211222/whd3lgcfxnh4jaxelx54menfia.html//, accessed 28 January 2022.

Santamaría, Í. and X. Martínez, *Desde* Al Sur del Pacífico *hasta* Más allá de la Luna: *casi 6 décadas de teatro musical en España*, 3 vols. (Gráficas EUJOA S.A., 2016).

Savirón, E. '*West Side Story*: El Musical: Comentario', *agolpedeefecto.com*, 18 October 2018.

Serrano, D. [adaptor], *West Side Story: Libreto y canciones*. Basado en un idea de Jerome Robbins. Libreto de Arthur Laurents. Música de Leonard Bernstein. Letras de Stephen Sondheim. Una producción original dirigida y coreografiada por Jerome Robbins. ([Madrid: SOM Produce, 2018]).

Shakespeare, W. *Romeo and Juliet* and A. Laurents, L. Bernstein, S. Sondheim, and J. Robbins, *West Side Story* (New York: Dell Publishing Co., Inc., 1965).

Sierra, P. 'Un clásico musical todavía vivo', *El País*, 9 October 1983, p. 53.

Simeone, N. *Leonard Bernstein*: *West Side Story* (Farnham, UK: Ashgate Publishing Limited, 2009).

Sopeña, F. 'Bernstein: el mito', *Diario de Mallorca*, 10 January 1988, p. 40.

'Steven Spielberg Dishes on Making a Musical with *West Side Story*', https://nofilmschool.com/spielberg-makes-west-side-story, accessed 21 January 2022.

Subirana, J. 'Sueños de candilejas', *El Periódico de Catalunya*, 7 May 1996, p. 58.

Tallerico, B. '*West Side Story*,' www.rogerebert.com/reviews/west-side-story-movie-review-2021, accessed 22 January 2022.

The Stage Company, 'Gaby Goldman', http://thestagecompany.com.ar/gaby-goldman/, accessed 1 November 2020.

Torres, M. '*West Side Story* se presenta en Madrid con la coreografía de Jerome Robbins', *El País*, 5 October 1983, https://elpais.com/diario/1983/10/06/cultura/434242812_850215.html, accessed 27 September 2020.

'TVE: Homenaje a Bernstein en su 70 cumpleaños', *Diario de Avisos*, 28 August 1988, p. 47.

Vendrell, R. 'Los Sharks y los Jets se enfrentan en el Tívoli', *El Periódico de Catalunya*, 24 November 1996, p. 56.

Vidales, R. 'El Bernstein más pegadizo', *ElPais.com*, 20 October 2018.

Villegas, M. 'Ante *West Side Story*: El extraño caso del musical', *Film Ideal*, 116, 15 March 1963, pp. 178–79.

'*West Side Story*', www.eldoblaje.com/datos/FichaPelicula.asp?id=65328, accessed 28 January 2022.

'*West Side Story*: Birth of a Classic', Library of Congress [website], www.loc .gov/exhibits/westsidestory/westsidestory-legacy.html, accessed 12 July 2021.

'*West Side Story: The New Broadway Cast Recording*' (Masterworks Broadway 88697–53085–2, 2009).

'*West Side Story* (1961): Release Info', IMDb, www.imdb.com/title/tt0055614/ releaseinfo, accessed 12 July 2021.

'*West Side Story* como nunca se ha visto en Madrid', *TopCultural.es*, 4 October 2018.

'*West Side Story* de Steven Spielberg/Nuevo Tráiler Oficial', www.youtube .com/watch?v=sx3_DqF-14s, accessed 28 January 2022.

'*West Side Story* de Steven Spielberg/Nuevo Tráiler Oficial', www.youtube .com/watch?v=Q2Pg67Hfz3Q, accessed 28 January 2022.

'*West Side Story* llega al Auditorium', *Diario de Mallorca,* 22 February 1998, p. 24.

'*West Side Story* vuelve al cine por un día', *Fotogramas*, 5 December 2012, www.fotogramas.es/noticias-cine/a495785/west-side-story-vuelve-al-cine-por-un-dia/, accessed 12 July 2021.

'*West Side Story*, una historia de Nueva York, llega a la escena de Madrid', *Faro de Vigo*, 13 December 1997, p. 72.

Whitten, S. 'With just $36.6 million in ticket sales, *West Side Story* is officially a box-office bomb', www.cnbc.com/2021/12/26/west-side-story-is-officially-a-box-office-bomb.html, 26 December 2021, accessed 22 January 2022.

Winkels, E. 'España baila al ritmo de oro', *El Periódico de Catalunya*, 3 August 1996, p. 26.

www.forocoches.com/foro/showthread.php?t=8876794, accessed 28 January 2022.

www.foroseldoblaje.com/foro/viewtopic.php?t=83210, accessed 28 January 2022.

www.ibdb.com, accessed 11–13 October 2020.

www.mtishows.com/west-side-story, accessed 1 November 2020.

www.westsidestory.es/, accessed 1 November 2020.

Zorrilla, V. 'Hay Poca Atención al Teatro', *Cambio 16*, 26 January 1998, p. 76.

Cambridge Elements ☰

Musical Theatre

William A. Everett

University of Missouri-Kansas City

William A. Everett, PhD is Curators' Distinguished Professor of Musicology at the University of Missouri-Kansas City Conservatory, where he teaches courses ranging from medieval music to contemporary musical theatre. His publications include monographs on operetta composers Sigmund Romberg and Rudolf Friml and a history of the Kansas City Philharmonic Orchestra. He is contributing co-editor of the *Cambridge Companion to the Musical* and the *Palgrave Handbook of Musical Theatre Producers*. Current research topics include race, ethnicity and the musical, and London musical theatre during the 1890s.

About the Series

Elements in Musical Theatre focus on either some sort of 'journey' and its resulting dialogue, or on theoretical issues. Since many musicals follow a quest model (a character goes in search of something), the idea of a journey aligns closely to a core narrative in musical theatre. Journeys can be, for example, geographic (across bodies of water or land masses), temporal (setting musicals in a different time period than the time of its creation), generic (from one genre to another), or personal (characters in search of some sort of fulfilment). Theoretical issues may include topics relevant to the emerging scholarship on musical theatre from a global perspective and can address social, cultural, analytical, and aesthetic perspectives.

Cambridge Elements ≡

Musical Theatre

Elements in the Series

A full series listing is available at: www.cambridge.org/EIMT

CPSIA information can be obtained
at www.ICGtesting.com
Printed in the USA
BVHW031743060722
641479BV00005B/24